MIN
BROKEN HEART

SELF-COMPASSION FOR NEGATIVE MIND-STATES

JACKIE HAWKEN

MINDFULNESS
BRISTOL

www.mindfulnessbristol.co.uk

© Jackie Hawken 2015

SECTION ONE

IMPORTANT ELEMENTS
AT THE BEGINNING

*"All meditation must arise from
compassion and love."*

Akong Rinpoche, Samye Ling

To Paul
Enjoy your
Mindful journey
Love Jackie
x

Dedication

To Chöje Akong Tulku Rinpoche*

My guiding light
My precious, generous, egoless perfect teacher
You gave me stillness
You guide me still
My life has meaning because of you

*The Head of the Karma Kagyu Lineage, H H The Karmapa declared Akong Rinpoche, who passed away on 8th October 2013, to be a Dharmacharya – "One who teaches the dharma by example" – he embodied Mindfulness in action, demonstrating compassion to the very highest degree. He did not seek the limelight, quite the reverse. He manifested total impartiality and generosity of spirit and as such was a truly enlightened being.

Thanks

Thank you to Coleman Barks, who has enriched our lives by translating the works of Rumi and who gave me permission to use 'The Guest House' and a verse from 'The mouse and the camel'; and Tara Brach who has written one of my favourite books 'Radical Acceptance', who gave me permission to adapt a wonderful exercise from her book. I humbly appreciate their generosity.

Eternal thanks to Akong Rinpoche – to whom this book is dedicated – and Lama Yeshe Rinpoche, who both encouraged me to teach Buddhism and Mindfulness, knowing what a flawed human being I am. Their very presence in my life enriches it beyond measure.

Thank you, Ellie, my beautiful daughter, who persuaded me to write this book, my son Dimitri who has taught me a lot about myself and Alfie the Wonderdog – my faithful and loving companion.

Grateful thanks go to my many patient friends who supported me during my dark night of the soul and in particular Toni, who counselled me so well, Tony, Steve and John who ensured I maintained my faith in men by being lovely mates, Julie who provided so many opportunities to enjoy myself during the dark days, Susie and Colin who provided the home from home I needed, Belinda – always so kind to her crazy neighbour, Donna who despite the fact we have not yet met gave me unconditional support and empathetic feedback on the forum we both joined, Cathi who wrote 'Mad Cow' and Adrilia, who received many e mails full of pain, always patiently responding in this exceptional way:

"I am sorry you are still hurting so very much, but I can see and feel the healing process: it is one of great courage in which you are facing things and seeing the demons clearly and facing the fear ... and this is what's needed to finally get past all of it. This is how the fears lose their battle - when we can see them squarely and say 'I see you, move over! Now let's get on with this show!' The rest of your life is just beginning ... which is why Spirit stepped in to free you, so that you can begin your new life and your new work."

Blue Fire of Grief

Come to the fire, he said.
But she was afraid.
Come to the fire, he said.
So she flew and joined her tribe.

She did not feel worthy.
Her heart was closed.
She lived in fear and grief,
Carrying on her face the rictus of the Joker.
Joy long being absent,
The romance she believed in was nothing more than
bait

So she came to the fire,
Discovering all this and more –
That her grief had come from anger and
abandonment,
Slowly morphing into depression.
And the numbness was frozen fear.

Yes, she came to the fire,
Listening to his soft sweet words;
Telling her to trust her heart voice,
And surrender to her fear,
Connecting to herself.

He told her she would feel alive
By expressing her imbalance,
Accepting the slow speed of recovery from grief.

So she surrendered,

Surrendered to love.
Held in the blue waters of whispering mother
Saskawhihiwine,
Drawing in her divine breath.

Returning to her homeland,
She knew she would be well.
Because she loves oak.
It is her favourite tree –
Grounding her:
Manifesting her slow strong growth towards healing

*Written by Jackie Hawken (while celebrating her 60th birthday
at the Blue Deer Centre, Upstate New York, in August 2012)
after listening to Grandfather Fire's teachings on grief*

CONTENTS

Dark nights of the soul and darker mornings of despair
Rumination
Obsessing and cognitive dissonance
Is it love or compulsion/addiction/codependence?
Shock
Loneliness and learning to be alone
Anxiety
Anger / Rage
Hatred
Grief

SECTION FOUR – Rebuilding your Self page 78

The positive aspect of being 'discarded' & the 'shaman's death'
Appreciating when a romantic relationship is no longer good for you
Channel PAIN into helping others
Healing your heart
Closure
Obsession
True change
Strong attachment
Self-esteem
Regrets
Acceptance
How to deal with unwanted thoughts
A Mindful approach to forgiveness
Rebuilding and self-love
The reality check-list

About the exercises and recommended approach

List of Mindfulness Exercises

1 – Sitting by the stream
2 – A basic Mindfulness sitting practice
3 – 5-minute Mindfulness practice
4 – 3 deep Mindful breaths
5 – Breathing in a healing colour to the whole of your body
6 – Being with your pebble
7 – Day-breaks
8 – Embracing the inevitable: experiencing true acceptance

SECTION SEVEN – More information at the end
page 175

Prologue

"On a human level, there can be misunderstandings: if our ego is in the way we cannot admit mistakes. Our responsibility to others is to practice compassion to those who do you wrong. You say: 'It must be my past karma. May I forgive them'. It is a very high compassion threshold. Whenever you can, think more positively rather than focus on anger or revenge. If you sit and let fear come and go it has no seed to grow. If you dig it up and analyse it, it will grow."

Akong Rinpoche, Samye Ling

A few years ago, the sun was shining over the beautiful Holy Isle in Scotland for the entire week of a Mindfulness retreat and for most people it would have felt like paradise. Sadly, I was struggling with very powerful negative feelings because of the destructive relationship I had come out of with a man with Narcissistic Personality Disorder. I had gone through the predictable experience of being love-bombed and put on a pedestal, followed by the inevitable devalue and discard. The pain and emptiness was killing me.

Rinpoche had told me to 'Let him go – let him sort his own problems out. I want you to study Mindfulness so that you can teach and help people'. You never ignored Rinpoche's advice and so I started my studies in Mindfulness a few weeks later. I was not to know that this was the greatest gift that he could have given me – it has changed my life.

As I sat in the meditation room at Holy Isle with my mind whizzing around like a washing machine on spin cycle, I was screaming in my head 'Let it go, let it go, let it go'... Suddenly there was a word change – replacing 'go' with 'be' created an immediate shift. Yes, let it be. Let it all be. There is nothing I can do so I might as well put down the burden rather than struggle with pushing it away. LET IT BE!

I have always struggled with the expressions 'other half' 'better half' 'soul mate' or 'love of my life'. For me, it implies a lack of wholeness within the self. When people 'lose their hearts' they often lose their minds. Misguidedly treating the narcissistic ex as 'the love of my life' meant I loved him with ALL of my life, not keeping anything for myself, coming close to spiritual, emotional and physical death. I was to learn that it was a pattern of mine.

I believe that when people get together to experience a 'romantic relationship', three levels are in operation:

- Top, visible level of what others see "They make such a good couple."
- Middle level: "I am with him because I love him. I am so lucky." and *vice versa.*
- The bottom, unconscious level, e.g. Her: "I will give everything to him because he will stay with me." Him: "This is a woman who has a lot to give me so I will stick around until I have sucked all her energy and can replace her with fresh supply."

Obviously, the third, hidden layer is the *real* reason why people get together (but they are not even aware of it). If that reason is not healthy, the relationship will ultimately flounder.

When a relationship ends, the ensuing heartbreak can be overwhelming – reframing even the most stable life into a seemingly unchangeable mess. It is when we realise that happiness is within us, and that so many of us look to romantic relationships to feel validated, happy and loved – with the attendant risks and potential heartbreak – that we can finally heal. We may even learn that the way we love is a form of self-abuse.

As a Buddhist, I was very fortunate to have my beloved teacher, Akong Rinpoche, to ask for advice. Buddhist thought advocates a practice "Take all blames into one" – a way of seeing our own responsibility in the matter. For, as difficult as it is to get our head around, we have played a part in the 'failure' of the relationship – whether it is choosing someone who aligns with your need to give (as a co-dependent personality) or to confirm that you are not worth very much (as in the case of someone with very low self esteem).

As a child I learnt early on to take care of others. My toxic partner, a weak and needy man, was the perfect person to take care of. I was repeating a pattern. When he had sucked all the life force out of me and replaced me with the next supply source, I touched the void and had to work very hard to come back from it. I now realise that I was suffering with low self esteem and a co-dependent personality most of my life, so you can imagine the sort of men I attracted - toxic relationships where the man took and took until I was empty: but my part in it was as someone who *had* to give and give until I was empty! I was complicit – blaming the other in dysfunctional relationships is not at all helpful. We need to understand how to develop personal responsibility, not give our power away to others.

The Universe – that sends you the same lesson until you learn it – seeing that I was not learning the lessons of my co-dependent attitude in relationships, decided to hit me so hard that I was forced to face up to it. Because of my childhood experiences, my greatest fears were of betrayal, abandonment and annihilation. This was the worst that could happen. Well, the worst happened: I am still *here*, and I never have to go *there* again. By being forced, by the experience, to face my fears and be truly alone, I discovered the true meaning of 'what doesn't kill you makes you stronger.'

During my recovery, I joined a forum for women recovering from narcissistic abuse and met some lovely mutually-supportive people. I decided to give up alcohol, which was affecting my liver and giving me migraines (when I was with the ex we drank too much together as he insisted on having what he called 'wine o'clock' every day). I was not in a hurry to look for another 'romantic' relationship and I learnt not to waste time on psychic vampires any more.

As a psychological coach, I have attracted a number of clients who have been/are going through this 'soul rape', and because I have had this experience I have the aptitude and confidence to work with them: I see positive results and it fulfils my Buddhist path. I have learnt, with the help of Mindfulness, to find joy in the small things in life. Walking in nature with Alfie gives me immense happiness.

I now give myself permission to do things for myself. I recognise the people that I have invited in to be negative forces in my life and now obey my own mantra *"I choose to spend time with people around whom I feel good about myself"* (stated in the positive, owning my responsibility for my life and taking back my power).

So what have YOU found positive in your suffering? This is not to denigrate our suffering or the vileness of what we may have been through. It is simply to say that finding something positive from the experience means we can reclaim our power, learn lessons, and give ourselves permission, finally, to be happy. When the worst has happened, what have you got to lose? You can take some risks in life – really go for it.

Maybe in the relationship you ignored the warning bells, or 'red flags'. We *fall* in love (and sometimes land on our faces), but what we need is to *grow* and *thrive* in love instead. We 'fall madly' in love and can become 'mad' as a result. We are left with fog and confusion because we trusted someone with our heart and they trashed it. Now you have to learn to be your own best friend. To recover, you must stay away from your ex, keeping the bad behaviour front and centre initially, so that you don't go back. Forgiveness comes later. You have possibly had psychological trauma to your brain and body. Psychological pain is horrific – one of the most stressful experiences of your life.

While on Holy Isle, my Mindfulness professor remarked: "One day you will thank him from the bottom of your heart". He was right – the ex didn't intend to give me such a gift but that is what happened. Hitting rock bottom, I was finally forced to learn to be in a loving, respectful relationship with myself. I have never been happier, secure in the knowledge that I am loved and loving and that it doesn't matter where the love comes from. And Mindfulness is the glue that sticks all this together.

This book is for people who have suffered heartbreak. It is mainly for people who have had their heart broken in either an ordinary or toxic relationship: and the exercises can also help people whose heart has been broken by all other losses a human being can experience. There is no easy remedy: You HAVE to go through it, but Mindfulness helps us all, in all situations. There is not a moment in our lives when we cannot practise Mindfulness.

Advisement

Modern-day Mindfulness is taught in a secular way – appealing to all faiths and none. Mindfulness was taught by the Buddha over two and a half thousand years ago, and is the 7th in the Noble 8-fold Path of Buddhism. Many of the people who teach Mindfulness, me included, are Buddhists. Buddhists do not want to 'convert' people to their way of life. Indeed, the Dalai Lama says that in order to avoid conflict we almost need as many religions as people in the world. Being on the Buddhist path of self-responsibility, as well as having my relationship with my precious Tibetan teacher, informs my work and my entire life. So from time to time I mention Buddhism and Buddhists in this book. Despite the modern secular way of teaching Mindfulness, I cannot 'eliminate' all mention of Buddhism. If the reader is uncomfortable with this, I do not apologise.

I have qualifications and experience in many areas but I do not consider myself to be an expert in any of them. This book is written from the heart, from my knowledge and experience. If anything resonates with you and you are experiencing very low mood, please do consult a doctor/psychologist/coach/healer or anyone else you trust who can help to guide you with your recovery. Please do not suffer in silence or avoid medical help. When I was suffering, I spent a lot of money (and I don't regret it) seeking help from many different people, putting together the pieces of my story as well as of my soul and my broken heart. Good luck, you will get there – please be patient. It took me four years to recover and each step was an experience – as my Tibetan teachers would say: "Baby steps, one foot in front of the other."

Introduction to this book

"When relationships break up, people become angry. The attachment is very strong... and there is always pain: that is what you have to go through."
Akong Rinpoche, teaching in the Temple at Samye Ling.

This book is a result of my own journey from pain to power, self-discovery, self-responsibility, self-love and self-acceptance, using Mindfulness. Throughout, I refer to some of the 26 exercises in Section 6 of this book, which offer us a way to be in the present moment, allowing our feelings and ourselves to just *be*. **Exercises 6** and **24** are an efficient way to learn how we focus using Mindfulness.

Within the book, there is a large emphasis on the negative mind-states that are associated with heartbreak: the reason for this is two-fold:

- When we are going through the upset at the end of a relationship, whether toxic or ordinary, our thoughts can be very repetitive. This book reflects that by emphasising in different ways what we can experience. The

27

exercises assist us to combat what life throws at us.

- Mindfulness involves recognising what is going on in our minds, and allowing ourselves to BE. The more we understand thoughts, emotions and feelings and the way the 'stream' flows through our mind 24 hours a day, the more we can see thoughts and emotions as fleeting episodes, not fixed mind-states.

Recovery is like peeling back the layers of an onion: apart from the inevitable tears (that can be cathartic and healing), once we accept the challenge of the journey and the fact that we have no choice but to move forward, changes occur as we become stronger. We engage so much with what we *think*. This book points out what those thoughts can be and how they can affect us.

You will see that putting emphasis on self-love will help you recover: sometimes we need some time on our own to find our equilibrium, rather than constantly relying on being 'loved' by someone else. I hope I can persuade you to try taking all the love you feel capable of giving to another and GIVE IT TO YOURSELF! It is not selfish and nor is it isolating: it is empowering and makes sense. The real alchemical journey with heartbreak is finding and recognising who you are. As Adrilia said to me:

"You may be mad as hell and you don't want to let go of him, even now. But you must. You have been there and done that. You mustn't kid yourself that you could have changed him or healed him We all feel the weariness. And given what has happened, this is the time to feel weary. But it passes. And it will pass because you are a captivating, juicy, delicious, vibrant, loving, woman who is full of Life and full of Love of Life."

SECTION TWO

SOME DEFINITIONS AS THEY APPLY TO THIS BOOK

"Meditation doesn't mean to change yourself but to BE your mind within your body. If you bring your mind into your body it doesn't matter if your thoughts are good or bad because there is no such thing as good or bad thoughts. Simply treat all thoughts the same. In meditation you don't DO anything. Sometimes when meditating you want to get rid of your thoughts, but you must just accept them, then they dissolve by themselves. Meditation can therefore be both simple and difficult. It is important to meditate without expectations. Expectations are an obstacle in your practice."

Akong Rinpoche, teaching in the Temple at Samye Ling

Mindfulness – its origins and how it works

In Buddhism, the four highest emotions are said to be loving-kindness, compassion, sympathetic joy and equanimity. These emotions lead to genuine happiness if they are practised in our daily lives.

Mindfulness Meditation is a western, secular, form of meditation derived from Buddhist Insight Meditation, where we develop the skill of paying attention to what is happening, while it is happening with self-acceptance and self-compassion, using the breath as an anchor. Through practising it, we become more able to express the higher emotions and are less stuck in troubling emotions.

Mindfulness is something we can do 24 hours a day, because whatever we are doing we can do it *Mindfully* – enjoying and focussing on the present without constantly having our bodies in one place and our minds focussed on the past or the future. I ask people, do you ROW with yourself? Do you Ruminate over the past, Obsess in the present or

Worry about the future? Of course you do! Get to know yourself – **Exercise 25** and **Exercise 26** are two small exercises to help you focus.

We observe how distracted the mind can be and how the constant stream of images, sensations, thoughts and feelings flowing through our brain-mind call for our attention. When we, as the watcher, realise that we have been distracted, we return to the awareness of our breath with kindness and acceptance and maybe a dose of curiosity about how we function. As we begin to live more fully in the present by cultivating Mindfulness, we learn to let go of unhelpful, habitual mind-states that cause us difficulties and unhappiness.

Practising Mindfulness leads to more resilience, a happier and calmer attitude and an increase in psychological and physical wellbeing. With openness and acceptance, we can learn to use Mindfulness every day, throughout the day, in order to deal with our tricky minds. With heartbreak, the inevitable obsessive thinking can be very destructive. By using Mindfulness techniques we succeed in becoming more stable and optimistic – it takes time and effort and it works: like a muscle, it needs to be exercised! **Exercise 2** introduces you to a basic sitting practice.

Mindfulness is not just meditation. Mindfulness is a way of living that involves being as PRESENT as we can be, as often as possible. A wonderful way of doing this is to sit in a garden, listening to the birds, looking at the flowers, feeling the sun on our body, breathing all the way in to our stomach area and feeling the groundedness of being on the spot. This is Mindfulness. **Exercise 19** is helpful with this.

Heartbreak can bring anxiety, despair, disturbance to our eating and sleeping patterns and obsessive thoughts. The grieving process continues for a long time. The wound takes a long time to heal and the psychological scar is always there as a reminder.

In Buddhism, we refer to the "genuine heart of sadness" and the final verse of the Rumi poetry I use in **Exercise 9** really encapsulates this sentiment for me. With heartache, feeling so raw and vulnerable, opening your heart to the pain is, incredibly, one of the most useful things you can do. From the depth of our suffering we can rise like a phoenix and recognise that, as Rumi says: "Your loving doesn't know majesty until it knows its helplessness."

When I became a Buddhist it was with the knowledge that I was finding a purpose and a path. If we see our lives as a journey and that the final, inevitable and inescapable destination is death, it may help us to concentrate more on enjoying that journey. **Exercise 14** is a useful reminder!

Insight

Buddhist teachings tell us that the mind is both the source of our happiness and our suffering. Once we accept this, we realise that it is all up to us. When I was suffering with heartbreak, with the help of my intellectual understanding I realised that I could not get rid of my rumination or my depression by suppressing it. This is where the RAIN exercise was, and is, so important to me. So many of us try to suppress thoughts and emotions, buying into the stratagem of 'positive thinking', only to end up beating ourselves up because it doesn't 'work'. **Exercise 11** was useful in helping me sleep.

Self-blame arises from low self-esteem. Low self esteem results in a victim mentality, fear of asserting oneself and an addiction to people-pleasing. By Mindfully observing what our self-talk is, we can change the habitual tendencies.

The essence of Mindfulness is to allow you to be fully present and relate to what is happening in your life – 'good' and 'bad' – while it is happening. In a conversation with Akong Rinpoche, he told me that I should integrate a Mindful state into my everyday existence. This advice is my anchor.

Self-compassion

"Develop limitless compassion to whoever is around you, including those who cause you pain and suffering or who cause you joy. You must try to be useful. If you are not Mindful, you are not useful. For example, tidying cushions in the shrine room – you may not put them in a useful place – you must be Mindful. It is important that you have limitless compassion, especially towards those under your authority such as children, cats etc. You must be kind and gentle and take care of others. You cannot change the whole world but you can change yourself. Take the shrine room into your mind so it is always at peace. Be Mindful on your journey home."

Akong Rinpoche, teaching in the Temple at Samye Ling, 2001.

In his talks, the Dalai Lama defines compassion as a wish that we, and others, be free from suffering. He says that if we want others to be happy, we should practice compassion and that if we want to be happy ourselves we should, again, practice compassion! Compassion includes the ability to be warm, supportive, kind, sensitive and empathetic, including to ourselves.

The Buddha said that the cultivation of loving-kindness and compassion is 'all of the practice'. These are skills that we can develop and strengthen. He further said that when we resist pain it makes matters worse. We need to discover a way in which we will be free from unnecessary suffering.

Compassion is the antidote to the poison of anger. We can face our pain – both psychological and physical – and respond with self-compassion and self-understanding. By simply following our breath all the way in and all the way out we develop genuine sympathy towards ourselves.

It is really important to remind ourselves what self-compassion is not: It is not self-indulgence or selfishness. It *is* an essential life-skill for a happy life. **Exercise 13** is helpful.

I learnt about grasping and aversion in the most destructive way possible (according to the Dalai Lama): in my head. As bad news accumulated at the end of my relationship, I descended into depression and misery. The rumination which plagued my every waking (and seemingly sleeping) hour continued unabated, reinforced by my negative thinking. The wish I had had for many years to be 'serene' was slipping ever further from my grasp.

I was not compassionate to myself when I 'failed' to be able to meditate, but unbeknownst to me, the Mindfulness practices were seeping into my unconscious as I studied and taught. My favourite Mindfulness exercise was then – and is now – The Guest House and RAIN which I have mentioned before. My guests were resentment, anger, hatred, fear, annihilation, stuckness and a desire for revenge. As ugly as they were, they were *my* guests and slowly, slowly, I learned to live with their frequent visits. My life depended on learning this stuff.

Listening to the words of the Dalai Lama I finally and really comprehended how self-destructive I was being. He reminds us that powerful emotions such as hatred, anger and desire (all of which I was feeling, much to my self-disgust and lack of self-compassion) will not bring us long-lasting happiness and can cause us physical harm. He also says that when we have difficulty in our lives, it is an opportunity to gain inner strength. In his compassionate way, he tells us that we should not limit 'meditation' simply to formal sessions, which echoes what Akong Rinpoche said: "I want you to practice Mindfulness all day every day."

Love

It doesn't matter where the love comes from. Anon

The Oxford English Dictionary describes 'love' as: a strong feeling of affection – as a noun; to feel deep affection or sexual attraction for someone; an affectionate greeting (especially in my home city of Bristol!)

Sexual love is nature's way of tricking people into producing the next generation. It can be intense and powerful. When love is returned you feel happy; if not, you can be miserable. It is a risk. As someone once said to me: "Love means giving another the power to destroy you and trusting them not to". It makes you vulnerable and can be a blessing or a curse. There is a thin line between love and hate and the opposite of love is not hate, it is indifference.

Neuroscientists have shown that when romantic love crashes down, the result is like a trauma to the brain. With the brain-mind and body connection, heartbreak can lead to physical as well as mental illness. When people are 'crazy in love' certain hormones are produced and when the heart is broken, the withdrawal can be as serious as from drug-addiction. Some people can be addicted to love, to the hormones generated when they fall *madly* in love. Many of us have bought into the saying 'love makes the world go round' but what type of love: sexual, romantic love or love for a child, a friend, a dog, or all sentient beings?

When we believe we are in love with someone who reciprocates, it could be that they love you for what you give, rather than what you share. Equally, you could see them through the prism of what *you* are and what you can give, reflected back to you through your projection rather than actually seeing them for who they are. It is complicated! As wise Adrilia said:

"I am sorry you don't believe you can trust a man again, but at the same time I respect your truth and your honesty about the whole thing. And I do see that there comes a time when we treasure our freedom and our friends and we realize how blessed we are ... having so much and so many beautiful people in our life ... and so much magic and healing and mystery and health and skill .. and work to be done ... that a relationship with a man becomes something you can take, and also something you can definitely leave and not become tangled up in."

Heartbreak

The Oxford English dictionary defines a broken heart as 'A state of extreme grief or sorrow typically caused by the death of a loved one or the ending of a romantic relationship.'

The agony of a broken heart can be excruciating. It can feel like your heart was ripped out of your chest and stomped on, so you cannot breathe. Time can heal and so can actively working through the pain. Often, needs that were not met as a child are awakened by the wound we experience and it can feel unbearable.

WHAT are you broken-hearted about? Often it is a loss from childhood that has been suppressed, not dealt with and resurrected. Our unconscious has a 'default position' to which we return again and again. Understanding what this is (e.g. abandoned child, victim, angry person, guilty person...) means that we can learn to recognise and deal with it. When someone does a total turnaround on previously expressed 'true love' and plans, this can lead to confusion, disappointment and pain. We may blame ourselves and then fall into our old, familiar, default position.

There are many reasons for a broken heart and there are 3 main losses involving other sentient beings:

- The loss of a person/beloved animal through death
- The loss of an ordinary ('normal') relationship
- The loss of a 'toxic' relationship (often with someone with a 'Cluster B' personality disorder).

In an ideal world, we would all be attracted to someone who is constant and genuine, but many of us commit to the 'wrong person' and suffer the consequences. If you have a personality which attracts people who will use and abuse you, this suffering will continue to occur until you learn (and some people never do). It is important that we learn to process our feelings rather than suppress them so that they burst out like a pressure cooker when we least expect it. We need to learn to LET IT BE, rather than let it go!

If a 'romantic' relationship you have been in was an 'ordinary' relationship, you will suffer a lot less than if you have been in a toxic relationship. There are many ways of describing a good relationship: for instance it could be one where you are not afraid to be yourself because you and your partner accept each other for who you really are; both of you want to work on making it successful and there is compatibility on most of the important levels – emotional, physical, sexual, mental, intellectual, spiritual and so on. More than anything, you are truly honest and dependable with each other. Sometimes relationships simply break down because people grow apart.

If the relationship was toxic, when it ends you may feel discredited, accused of being unstable because you have indeed been destabilised. Your family and friends may well not understand. During the relationship you may have slowly been 'erased' as you gave and gave and gave. If someone treats you badly, there is something wrong with them, not you. Normal people do not go around destroying others. Please do not be hard on yourself. So many intelligent people with a great awareness of psychopathology still make mistakes in their relationships. Nobody is immune. When the time is right, use **Exercise 16** to help yourself.

As Adrilia said to me:

"You are worthy of love, companionship, wild, passionate, ecstatic relationship. As you continue navigating and feeling and naming and ranting and raving in your healing process ... remember who you are. Remember that vision of happiness and remember that you ARE worth it and that you will have that life and that relationship and that joy. You have been freed. It still hurts like hell, but it was necessary. The stakes were too high, and Spirit/Divine would not stand by and let you pour everything into a container that, after all, never wanted to be filled, patched up or healed."

Could you be a 'highly sensitive person' (HSP)?

One fifth of the population are said to be HSPs. Their characteristics include pronounced hypersensitivity and intuition, high empathy, attuned to the subtleties of where they are, conscientious and caring. They are very compassionate and empathetic, feeling other people's pain keenly and instinctively. People can take advantage of such personalities, who suffer in silence. HSPs feel such love and compassion for people that they believe their love can heal others. The others can respond with gratitude, but do they give back to them? If you are a HSP you may find heartbreak very difficult to cope with.

Our 'self' and our layers

I believe that each of us is somewhere on a spectrum from a 'zen' mind, through neurosis, to psychosis; add to that our character traits, our early childhood experiences and our adult experiences (and our past lives, if you believe in such things); then all of us have defence mechanisms which can be healthy or unhealthy, strong or weak. This is why the Dalai Lama maintains that there cannot be a 'one size fits all' approach to our wellbeing. Each of us is unique. Mindfulness isn't a 'one size fits all' either – it is the personal practice of allowing what arises to arise, learning to tolerate feelings and being as much as possible in the present moment.

Red flags for toxic relationships

"Depression is not a sign of weakness: it is a sign of being too strong for too long" Anon.

Toxic relationships can bring you very low mentally, emotionally and physically and lead to a breakdown. They are among the most devastating of all broken relationships. Some individuals can be charming, intelligent and highly manipulative, hiding the fact that the relationship, for them, will be about meeting their needs. Breaking up with them can mean coming to terms with the fact that the person you loved was not the person you were actually with and the relationship was nothing you thought it was. You need to find acceptance within yourself – real healing with learning and grieving. These relationships can damage your self-esteem, trust and ability to form healthy future relationships. It means something to you, not them.

People with Cluster B personalities, such as Narcissists, are incapable of mature empathic love. Hope dies slowly and painfully. They love in a childish way – simultaneously superior and dependent. But it is not real. It can be a relief when you understand what has happened: knowledge is power. You believe that they are needy individuals, but in reality they feel entitled. No matter how much you give, it won't be enough until you are completely drained. You need to learn to distance yourself emotionally and physically: walk away when 'negotiating' hasn't worked. Years later you could still be obsessing as these relationships can be addictive. This is where **Exercise 8** can be very helpful.

It can take a long time to recover from a toxic relationship. First of all, many people who are close to us who haven't experienced this are unable to offer us the support we need. They may believe that you should just 'get over it'. But we can't, because this isn't a normal end of relationship. It was like a hit and run. They destroy your soul, leave the scene of the crime and blame you. They usually move on very quickly to their next supply source (usually having the next person already lined up) and we are left feeling bereft and insignificant, questioning what is wrong with us and full of unexpressed rage.

It can take us a long time to want to be involved in a relationship again. First, we need to own and accept our feelings. But eventually we *will* recover and be stronger for it. Mindfulness is a marvellous remedy for this. **Exercise 15** is a good one to practice while you walk.

My view is this: we have experienced highs and lows out of the normal range and the shock is just too much to bear. We have given in to an illusion that we have finally met 'the one' and experienced the disillusionment, accompanied by a trigger of childhood fears of abandonment. So all in all, we have been in a head on car-crash of a relationship and we have got out alive, but only just.

Listen to your intuition. Your gut-mind might be telling you something your heart-mind and brain-mind haven't realised. When applied to relationships, we might ignore our 'inner tuition' at our peril. Someone may appear 'perfect' for us, yet we might feel uneasy. Pay attention to red flags! The Universe is always looking out for you.

Co-dependency

A co-dependent has often grown up in a dysfunctional family – a child who assumes responsibility for others and anticipates their needs, doing what they can to please everybody. A classic co-dependent is intelligent, hard-working and capable, needing constant validation and seeks peace within the self from outside the self (being defined by the view of others) and has difficulty saying 'No'.

Co-dependents can be addicted to the chemicals of grief, victimhood, despair, powerlessness, helplessness, anger and resentment; but the addiction is only a symptom. The cause is anxiety and emptiness caused by a childhood emotional wound – feeling the need for something outside of the self to rid them of the pain. They can lose their sense of self and identify, hiding the pain they feel, believing that they are responsible for everyone and that, being unworthy, if they help others (often to their own detriment) they will be loveable and people will stay with them.

The wounds/black holes in some people are attractive to those with a co-dependent personality. Many women see the 'little boy lost' in a man and want to help him. It feeds their ego, believing 'I can heal him'. Unfortunately, you can't heal someone like that – they can drain you and give you their depression. The effort to recover from this requires a painful 180 degree turn.

Co-dependents often experience 'high empathy': being so keen to identify with another's suffering that they become stressed, anxious and drained. A better state to be in is described as 'compassionate care' where we can be present for another person, without 'taking on' their issues and over-identifying with them.

Co-Dependents Anonymous is, according to their website 'A fellowship of men and women whose common purpose is to develop healthy relationships. The only requirement for membership is a desire for healthy and loving relationships'. CODA meetings are held all over the world and are run along the same lines as any 12-step programme. They maintain that co-dependency is an emotional and behavioural condition that is learned (usually in childhood) and affects the ability to have a healthy relationship with others.

Having discovered that I have a co-dependent personality, I attended some CODA meetings and learnt that co-dependents often suffer from denying their own feelings in order to help and be acceptable to others, low self-esteem, exaggerated loyalty and a need to control others (in order to feel safe).

Co-dependents focus on their romantic partner, to their detriment, forgetting what their own needs are.

They therefore attract unhealthy relationships, becoming absorbed with the needs of their (often narcissistic) partner, thus ensuring considerable suffering to themselves when the relationship ends.

This is why CODA meetings can be so helpful. Recovery of one's 'self' is very important and can lead to the serenity that a co-dependent has craved all their life, as well as resilience, workable self-esteem, self-worth and self-acceptance. It is then possible to put appropriate boundaries in place.

SECTION THREE

COMMON OBSTACLES AND CHALLENGING MIND-STATES

"You cannot escape your mind. Your shadow is with you all the time. The result depends on the effort you make... If you have birth, you have death. We must understand impermanence. We breathe in and out. Between our first and second breaths, time - and us - has changed. Therefore DO NOT CLING."

Akong Rinpoche, teaching in the Temple at Samye Ling.

The minefield of relationships

"If you think you are partly at fault, so be it. Forgive yourself. But also realize that that, too, is part of the story you had together ... part of that karma. It unfolded as it needed. It is complete. It was a relationship. Relationships are not perfect because people are not perfect ... But there are basic things and gifts that are exchanged ... and these are necessary for the wellbeing of both. Your relationship was one-sided ... You were giving it your all ... He was sharing what he could but mostly taking."
Adrilia

Sometimes relationships are a question of hope over experience! There is always the risk that romantic love can be a hoax. In order to be successful, people need emotional security and maturity, similar values and a willingness to work on the relationship. However, our primary relationship should *always* be with our own self. When we love, accept and forgive ourselves we can do it for others. See **Exercise 13.**

Everyone in life can be a spiritual teacher – for good or ill. When we meet a new person that we are attracted to, we are at risk of idealising them. We might believe that we understand each other instantly. But true intimacy comes with time. Projecting our desires onto a virtually unknown person involves illusion and disillusion. The word 'soul-mate' is bandied around. The other person may appear to be compatible with you because they are mirroring your desires, even your personality. You may sense 'instant compatibility'. Be aware! Be Mindful! Some people can be bad for you and the relationship can eventually reveal itself to be toxic.

Guardian angel or devil?

Do not make a partner your 'guardian angel'. Toxic partners often believe that they are superior and manifest grandiosity. We give them permission to be judge and jury over our existence. I fell for this and when my 'guardian angel' manifested the 'devil' that had been lurking there all along it was the worst pain imaginable. So take back your power. NEVER give your power to another person.

You cannot change others but you can change your response or attitude to them. You can only change YOU. So what choices are you making in relationships?

There can be a tendency to rush into relationships. Some people believe in 'love at first sight', 'whirlwind romances'. People confuse intensity with intimacy. These episodes can end in disappointment and unhappiness. Maybe you believe that you can follow your 'intuition' but actually it is not intuition but wishful thinking – the proverbial 'triumph of hope over experience'. 'Love at first sight' involves an emotional/chemical reaction. Losing our heart can also mean losing our head so that sometimes our mind breaks, along with our heart.

Being in a relationship where our needs are not met may become a habit for some of us. If we suppress our needs and hinder our growth we may be in conflict with our values and demonstrate a lack of boundaries. Without enough self-knowledge we may end up being too keen to have approval from – and give to – others, so that we can end up used, abused and angry.

When we seek validation from outside of ourselves, squashing our needs so that we are 'acceptable' we are left very vulnerable. Eventually, the end of a relationship may give you the spiritual boot up the backside that you need – to wake you up to where you are under-selling yourself and your needs. Remember, the Universe sends you the same lessons until you learn them.

You can, of course, go the other way and, finding yourself needy, expect that another person will change to fill your (non-expressed) needs. So a balance must be struck and the first step is to work towards being in a loving relationship with yourself, asking yourself what you need and going all-out to meet those needs, even if it is simply buying yourself flowers, going on a break to see a good friend, and so forth. Be Mindful whether you are honouring or neglecting your needs in a relationship. See **Exercise 20.**

Emotional vampires

Some people 'love' you or even 'befriend' you for the benefits they get. When the benefits stop, they leave. It wasn't love that hurt you but a person who didn't know how to love. Their 'story' is that you are a bad person so they don't need to be accountable for their behaviour. Unsurprisingly, when you have been vampirised you feel empty.

Emotional abuse and betrayal

Emotional abuse is often unconscious behaviour that is 'designed' to control and subjugate another human being through the use of fear, humiliation, intimidation, guilt, coercion or manipulation. Therefore it includes the emotional abuse from a toxic relationship.

Betrayal - whether in an ordinary or vampiric relationship - can be devastating. Trust disappears, to be replaced by very difficult feelings, including devastation if you didn't see it coming. Possible feelings of revenge may dominate. With a suitable lapse of time, forgiveness for yourself and the other person will help you move forward.

Acknowledge what your feelings are and ride the waves. Using Mindfulness, identify what the dominant feelings are, so that you can eventually gain some control over your emotions and make a decision as to what you wish to change in your life in order to hasten your recovery. And use **Exercise 15.**

Dark nights of the soul and darker mornings of despair

" 'I will be lonely' causes suffering and unhappiness. Many sufferings can end up as positive. If you have happiness you will also find suffering. Every suffering is to do with misunderstandings. Therefore ignore suffering and set aside time for meditation. Be gentle. It is how we treat children – kind but firm. One must work constantly to develop compassion – towards yourself, your friends and your enemies. Forgive the mistakes of yourself and others."

Akong Rinpoche, Samye Ling

You awake and you feel ok for a tenth of a second and then you realise why you do not feel ok. Your heart sinks low, the rumination is out of control, the fear and loneliness overwhelming. Often what we fear is that we will not be able to cope with what happens to us. If we could work on being in the moment and riding the waves of despair, that would help.

When an ordinary relationship comes to an end, we grieve the loss of our love affair and of the intimacy. We feel the pain of conflict. But with a toxic relationship, we have to deal with the discovery of the fact we have been through 'pedestal' (the over-valuation stage), devalue and discard. We may realise that we were just food and drink to a person who never truly loved us – they just adored what we gave them and how they felt being so loved by us. We also have the shock of the easy way that they move on to the next 'victim'. While we are left empty and grieving, they move on so easily. This then creates bitter angry feelings that we have to deal with, as well as the grief. With an ordinary relationship we can feel the poignancy of lost love. With a toxic relationship, we just feel loss.

When all else seems to fail, Mindfulness will help – just practising some of the exercises in this book will help you to soothe yourself in the darkest of times; such as **Exercises 5, 8, 12** and **21**. Running through all of the exercises in this book you will find the ones that you relate to – I have kept them all relatively short so that they are 'handleable'.

Rumination

You may refuse to let the relationship go because deep down you believe that it was your fault. This is an emotional, rather than intellectual, construct. Do you 'hate' yourself and think it was your fault? It wasn't and it isn't. You will eventually realise that you were freed from that situation!

Repetitively and obsessively focussing on the symptoms of distress is NOT a way of processing. It is stuck energy. It can go along with cognitive dissonance and PTSD. When we ruminate we keep an 'if only' narrative going on. We need to replace the 'what-ifs' with 'so-whats'. We ask ourselves "What did I do wrong?"

The bottom has fallen out of your world. You feel that you will never be happy again and thoughts of unworthiness and shame can lead to social isolation. Feelings of terror, annihilation and emptiness can arise. This can be linked to abandonment.

We can ruin the present moment by constantly going back to past hurts. On an intellectual level we know that there is no point in going over and over the past. The only usefulness is to educate yourself for the future. Look at, but don't dwell in, the past. Get out in nature, and practice **Exercises 1, 17, 18** and **19**.

Obsessing and cognitive dissonance

There is a difficulty in trying to hold two opposing thoughts or beliefs at the same time, endeavoring to make sense of a situation that makes no sense: "How can I love someone I also hate?" We find ourselves grappling with the memory of a person we no longer recognise because we fell in love with an illusion. Often we cannot get closure, particularly with a toxic relationship, but we help ourselves by making sure we process feelings. Eventually, we start to make sense of our 'story'. Self-compassion is very important at times like this. Things unfold at their own pace in their own time – we cannot force. If we are prone to negative self-talk we can use the CBT-inspired **Exercise 23.**

Is it love or compulsion/addiction/co-dependency?

It is not love that makes us want to go back to a toxic relationship. We want them back to fill the hole left by our 'stolen' heart. But no person should look for a relationship to fulfil their life. We may even stalk them on social media to try to work out what has happened and make sense of the chaos. But we can become obsessive and then ill. We keenly feel the loss of the good times, of having a partner, of sharing our life with someone. But what if that someone is ultimately not good for you? Use **Exercise 12 & Exercise 15** to help you with your broken heart.

Shock

When a dramatic shift occurs in our life such as the sudden end of a relationship, the emotional shock can paralyse us with fear/terror, anger, grief and resentment and we end up clinging to the past because we cannot imagine a happier present or future. This may lead to obsessive thoughts which increase our pain: add in rumination and our life can become unworkable. Mindfulness can help us to let go of the attachment to how we believe we want life to be and allow us to trust the potential for a better future. Stress can arise, creating an inability to manage our life. Sustained anger and stress is bad for your heart so getting out in nature and practising

Mindful walking is a necessary prescription to become well again. See **Exercise 10 & Exercise 17.**

Loneliness and learning to be alone

"Do not be afraid of loneliness. It is an opportunity to spend time with oneself" Tibetan Proverb

Loneliness grabs you: you feel like your entrails have been pulled out of you, at the same time as being gripped by a giant octopus that is squeezing the life out of every part of you.

We are the most important relationship we have and yet we so often shy away from spending time with ourselves. The society in which we have grown up places great value on being in a romantic relationship (just listen to the words of most contemporary songs); and if we are not, we feel we have 'failed' in some way. We may even be tempted to compromise and be in an unfulfilling relationship in order to look as if we are 'normal' and 'lovable' and to avoid the dreadful void of loneliness.

Yet by enjoying being alone, cultivating the relationship with oneself, discovering our own needs and wants, cultivating friendships and trying out new activities, we can better choose a relationship in which we can grow and thrive, because we don't *need* one.

Running away from loneliness and emptiness can lead people into toxic relationships. Being able to sit with these feelings in Mindful awareness is an essential part of relationship maturity. Learning to tolerate being alone enables us to develop the capacity to have a healthy and wholesome relationship with someone who is good for us. **Exercise 8** is helpful here.

It is important to remember that while some people need a romantic relationship, others are perfectly content to stay single. Many people live happily alone, with family, friends or pets. Choosing to be single, if only for a while, is a way to re-discover yourself, what makes you tick and what you might want in a future relationship. What is important is that we are comfortable with our life-choices and that we are not being coerced into living in a way that is not conducive to our wellbeing. So stop looking for ways to avoid alone-ness and start to embrace the time given you to develop a loving relationship with yourself. Wake up to **Exercise 26** and use **Exercise 25**.

Anxiety

It is part of the human condition. We can retrain our brain to respond to it. It often manifests by an overwhelming sense of apprehension and obsessive thoughts that you believe you cannot control. *But you can "control" how you respond.* Eventually, peace of mind will arise when you learn to allow your thoughts to flow in the stream of your consciousness, without clinging. Stare fear in the face, and the Universe will offer you support. Make **Exercise 3** your daily practice.

Anger/Rage

"When we are angry or have negative thoughts we need to grow the seed of compassion, like a tree."
Akong Rinpoche, Samye Ling, 2006.

When you see behind someone's mask and you realise the extent of their betrayal - shock, shame and sadness can give way to rage that comes in waves. It can be hideously consuming and needs an outlet, so to deal with it you need to use some form of physical exertion or helpful creative expression. Mindful acknowledgement and acceptance of rage is the first step towards processing it effectively. Get out and Mindfully walk – **Exercise 17.**

If you are stifling anger, first of all, allow it! It detects where we feel we have been mistreated. Maybe your partner shamed you into not expressing yourself. Years of stifling our feelings can result in depression (and eventually rage). Use a tennis racket to hit a pillow on your bed, running or vigorous walking. Use your anger appropriately! And then, as Akong Rinpoche suggests, start to grow the seed of compassion, for your suffering, for the suffering of others, recognise that you have developed a 'genuine heart of sadness' that connects you to the whole of humanity.

Hatred

"Never become bitter. Never lose your sense of humour." Audrey Betty Honeywell (my mother)

The Tibetan word for hatred is 'shedang' suggesting hostility from the depth of one's heart. Hatred doesn't affect our enemies – we are the ones who suffer because it eats us from within. Buddhism advocates loving kindness, compassion, sympathetic joy and equanimity and centres on release from delusion and suffering through meditation and receiving insight into the nature of reality. We can find peace of mind through daily Mindfulness practice – **Exercise 2**, and using RAIN, **Exercise 9**.

Grief

"Fear becomes paranoia. Grief becomes depression. Energetically, it is said that feeling 'nothing' is

intense fear. All energies have a speed to them. Happiness is fire, which is quick and hot. Grief is one of the slowest of the spiritual energetic processes. If you break up with someone, in traditional cultures they have the wisdom to know that grief is slow. Fear is far faster. Things must come back into balance. When grief arises, give way to it and be patient with yourself." Grandfather Fire, Blue Deer Centre, Upstate New York, 2012.

Your life is a mess and you are at an unbearably low point. You feel numb and the pain is excruciating. How do you begin again after you feel you have been destroyed? You must go through a grieving and healing process and you can only hide from the world for so long. Finding who you are is part of the journey. You may have been 'rejected' but its only one person. And you, too, have' rejected' people.

It is normal to grieve when we suffer loss. Although overwhelm can be difficult, we should not deny our pain. Grief is a natural process and it needs to be observed with compassion. Loss is disorientating and sick-making. Grief takes its own time. People can be stuck in grief for years. Mindfulness exercises help to 'loosen' the grip of grief, and provide a way of processing.

Having a breakdown does not have to be terminal. Think of it as shedding the old and walking towards the new, which is always scary; yet this too will pass. Yes, it is a nightmare but you *will* recover, you *will* be stronger. The experience of pain (physical and emotional), anguish and fear is very common. There is nothing wrong with you – this is often a normal part of the healing process. There is no way of escaping.

By Mindfully staying present with 'what is' and recognising that we can breathe in and out deeply and watch the 'television screen' of our mind as it rapidly flicks over, we can take the drama out of what we are feeling. If thoughts are plaguing you, remember that 'this too will pass' and keep a notepad close by, so you can write down whatever is coming up for you. Use **Exercises 1, 2** and **5.**

With the end of a relationship, the grief you experience can be 'ordinary' or catastrophic, depending on the relationship you are mourning. With a toxic relationship, *shock and disbelief* come first and then the inevitable *denial*, usually followed by *devastation and emptiness*. If the ex has a new 'love' we may also feel insanely *jealous* and *crazy*, leading to *anger*. On occasions, this can lead to excess drinking or even having mindless and unfulfilling sex which in turn exacerbates our feelings of extreme emptiness. Because we find the loss too hard to bear, we may be tempted to try *bargaining*.

Eventually we may educate ourselves about the different personalities we can get involved with and all of the 'red flags'. We may then become consumed by them and psychopathology, learning about love-bombing and 'gas-lighting' and all the other ways people can behave towards us. This can eventually lead to a feeling of extreme *rage* because we realise just how used and abused we can be. Unfortunately, *depression* can then follow, accompanied by a yo-

yoing of mood and constant rumination. We may have lost so much: self-respect, contact with friends, the ability to move ourselves forward...

Physically, there may be symptoms in some of our body organs. We need to heal. This might propel us to self-educate about toxic relationships and after that, practices such as Mindfulness can show us how to live better. We may join a forum and discuss our experiences with others who have been through 'love-bombing, pedestal, devalue and discard'. From this, we may well understand where we mistreated ourselves and how our low self-esteem led us into such a relationship. We start to take responsibility for how we allowed ourselves to be treated. We are not a victim. Eventually, our ability to feel happiness and joy returns. In fact, our life can improve. We eventually arrive at *acceptance,* but only after we have gone through a number of these other emotions, attitudes and feelings:

Loss, hurt, numbness, sadness, emptiness, misery, emotional outbursts, panic, guilt, loneliness, despair, despondency, yearning, obsessing, anxiety, idealizing, desire for revenge, struggling, disbelief, thoughts of suicide, difficulty with tasks, raw, vulnerable, self-doubt, feeling used and manipulated, feeling brainwashed, poor concentration, hopelessness, paranoia, obsession, going round in circles, rumination, helplessness, dread, tightness in your heart, short-lived euphoria, staying in bed, not washing, social isolation, withdrawal, stopping things that give you pleasure, crying, sobbing, IBS, a desperate need to 'go back', jealousy, inability to trust, chest pains, constant fight or flight feelings, weight gain/loss, skin issues, blame, self-blame, fear of the future, disgust, rage, shame, paralysed by pain, fear, terror, annihilation, confusion, disorientation, hatred, dependence, isolation, withdrawal, fear of future rejection, emotionally drained, sleeplessness.

With the Guest House & Rain, **Exercise 9,** you can entertain these visitors, eventually becoming adept at facing whatever life throws at you. And use **Exercise 22** to relax.

SECTION FOUR

REBUILDING YOUR SELF

"Deepen your connection to Buddhism. Be mindful all day every day. Turn negative into positive. Free yourself – do not go back to your partner. Use this opportunity to start Mindfulness training so that you can teach others and help them."

Akong Rinpoche, talking to me at Samye Ling, 2010

The positive aspect of being 'discarded' & the 'shaman's death'

"If your boyfriend has finished with you, rejoice for you are free!" Lama Yeshe Rinpoche, Samye Ling

While the end of a relationship has the capacity to bring us lower than we believe we can handle, it can also be the beginning of a new life. It is freedom, but not what we initially want. When ready, we could think: "Unlike you, I am capable of change and this is an opportunity I will seize". The drug of choice of an emotional vampire is attention. Slowly we can be freed from any brainwashing. We must not 'should' all over ourselves. We focussed on the other, not us. When we reject a toxic relationship, we escape. We were targeted because they wanted something from us. We found ourselves empty and no longer of use. It is time for us to learn to accept and love ourselves.

The metaphysical pain of a broken heart is one of the worst degrees of hurt felt. Recovery depends on length/type of relationship, whether it was ordinary or toxic, your personality and – importantly – your resilience. But remember – you *will* recover and it will allow you to begin your life again.

When we ride the waves of grief, the outcome can be a 'shaman's death' – at least that what was told I was going through when I was in the depths of despair. Indigenous populations who go through this initiation see the death as the dying away of the ego self, to be replaced by a connection to all things, aligning him or her with the will of the spirit world.

With a 'shaman's death', everything is shifting, changing and giving us the opportunity to be 'reborn'. In the process, we are becoming a completely new person with a bigger heart, more full of love and compassion, strength and confidence. It is important to trust in the divine and know that you are not alone. Often, this was what was so necessary and the reason why the stakes can be so high. You will emerge from this very difficult experience like the reborn phoenix -- healed, lighter, cleansed and transformed, with a new heart and new gifts. Even if you can't see how or why right now, trust that it is the very best outcome.

It is not always an easy process to face your demons and let go, but the 'divine' element in the experience makes this 'bitter medicine' easier to swallow. We are encouraged to make peace with our life experiences.

Appreciating when a romantic relationship is no longer good for you

There are two main reasons why a relationship might be toxic for you: first, because you are just not right for each other and you bounce off each other's issues; the second is because you are with someone with a personality disorder.

Discernment in relationships is a skill that many people take a long time to develop. They can be fulfilling but they can also be draining, stressful and imbalanced. When we observe this, there can be a tendency to ignore the warning signs and believe that it will get better of its own accord, which of course it will not. Relationships need respect, mutual caring and honest communication. If a passionate relationship does not have these elements then it might be time to consider leaving rather than let feelings fester and end up resentful and bitter when it inevitably ends.

Your heart is broken; but you are still alive. You know you are because you are still breathing. And that breath (the 'bridge' between your mind and your body, according to Thich Naht Hanh) will remind you that you are still here, still continuing. You walk into the woods, you continue to breathe. You hear the birds, you look at and touch the trees. One day at a time. One foot in front of the other. It is the only way. The use of small exercises, like **Exercise 4** and **Exercise 7** can be very helpful.

Channel PAIN into helping others

"These pains you feel are messengers – listen to them." Rumi

As stated, my precious teacher, Akong Rinpoche, told me to let my relationship go and help others instead. The capacity to heal others evolves naturally when you stop identifying yourself as a victim. Your pain gives you insight into the minds of people who have experienced heartache. Helping others can be restorative. I like to think of *emotional* PAIN as 'Processing Angst Intuitively Now'.

Healing your heart

When you are heartbroken you must learn to come out of the dark night of the soul, building up your strength before you leave the cocoon you have woven around your heart. 'Metamorphosis' in Greek means 'transformation' or 'change of shape'.

As I have said, the trauma of romantic loss can make you feel like your heart has been ripped out of your chest. It can even feel difficult to breathe. Our natural response is to try to suppress our feelings, our intense grief. But 'what you resist, persists'. While reflecting on the past makes you feel sad, thinking about the future makes you fearful and lonely. But being in the present moment, being Mindful, keeps you anchored. Stay present. Be aware of your feet on the floor, what you can see, hear, smell, taste and touch. Being in the present moment as often as possible, appreciating what is *here* helps us enormously. **Exercise 21** is useful.

The pain associated with heartbreak often comes in waves. You yo-yo from grief to a semblance of normality. This is a normal part of healing. No emotion stays with you forever. Breathing with present-moment awareness helps. It is important to be mindful about your health: the stress of heartache can take its toll on the body. Use calming herbs such as Tulsi (Holy Basil) to deal with the adrenaline rushes.

The end of a relationship involves a mixture of feelings. It is important to be gentle and kind with yourself. Take a pen and paper and write what you have learnt from the last relationship and what you would like in a future relationship. When you are suffering it is easy to forget that life goes on – this is a perfect opportunity for you to transform your life and move forward. Yes, there is loss, but there is also such a lot more to gain, including learning how you *can* handle your life and learn to be your own best friend. Use **Exercise 20.**

Closure

Sometimes we just have to accept that we may never have closure with a person, particularly if the relationship was toxic and we sensibly obey the 'No contact, no contact, no contact' rule. We might never have contact again (I did, 5 years on and was pleasantly surprised that I felt no anger, only indifference and at one point, compassion). What starts off as 'destruction' can actually turn out to be a source of healing (as in my case). Think: 'The Universe sends to me the ideal people for my life lessons and my greater good.'

Obsession

Why ruin your life obsessing over what your former partner is doing? Why are you doing it? Is it because you want him or her and their future partners to crash and burn? Leave it to karma. Any ruminating over it is self-destructive, negative to your SELF and gives YOUR power away to them. What do you want? If it is peace of mind then train your mind with Mindfulness – peace is a by-product of practising!

True change

Men and women who can change do it on their own. Outside of a relationship, we can work on our relationship with ourselves and any abandonment issues. So many people ricochet from one relationship to another, meaning they learn very little and never get past their issues or change for the better.

Strong attachment

In the Buddhist view the mind is located in the chest. 'A change of heart is a change of mind'. In Buddhism, the ultimate state of mind would be to have the same love for your enemy that you have for your child. I certainly can never see myself attaining that level of equanimity but it is good to keep it in mind and reflect upon the way that we are strongly attached to those we love and are hostile to our enemies: we may be projecting onto both. Therefore, when a loved one acts in a way we do not anticipate we could end up being seriously shocked. This emotional swing can destabilise us and cause us, and others, pain; hence the Buddha's teaching to practice equanimity.

Self-esteem

I define self-esteem as the internal relationship that we have with ourselves, and how we talk to ourselves. Low self-esteem is endemic in our society. I believe it is different from self-confidence, which is an external manifestation: the way we relate to others. Self-esteem is shaped by the strength of our resilience and our ability to ask to be treated in the way that we deserve and to feel comfortable expressing our needs. We can *decide* to change the way we look at ourselves and others and the way we live our lives. Mindfulness enables us to observe our negative self-talk. We can then learn to be assertive with others.

Regrets

People who work in palliative care are often struck by the things that the people they work with regret. Basically, when people get to the end of their lives it is not the amount of money they have that is the most important, or their work achievements. This should inspire us to live the lives we really want, not always putting work first, expressing our feelings courageously (what is the worst that can happen?), staying in touch with our friends and allowing ourselves to experience joy and happiness, having new experiences and being in the moment.

As a coach, when I get people to fill in the 'wheel of life' it amazes me the number of people who score themselves low on having fun. So consider this: Mindfully having fun in the present moment will radically change your life, ensuring that when you get to 100 you will not have so many regrets! See **Exercise 14**.

Acceptance

Acceptance is an integral part of living Mindfully; it is absolutely pivotal in 12-step programmes where every group ends with a prayer about acceptance. These groups encourage you to be wise about what you can – and cannot – change. Self-acceptance means freeing yourself from the need for approval from others. As stated in the prologue, having practised non-self-acceptance most of my life, giving my power away to others, my new mantra, (positively expressed) is: *"I choose to spend time with people around whom I feel good about myself."*

How to deal with unwanted thoughts

'Think positive' is something that we are urged to do. Therefore, when negative emotions arise, our natural tendency is to squash then, with the inevitable result of them surfacing again. If we allow ourselves to fully feel – in the moment – all the feelings and thoughts that arise, we are in a better relationship with ourselves. We can just let thoughts arise and then let them join the stream running through our brain-mind. We can also see them as clouds making their way slowly across the vast blue sky of our mind. We can allow this process, without squashing and without over-identifying. If we repress thoughts and emotions they get buried and surface when we least expect it. See **Exercise 2.** Use **Exercise 23** to handle negative self-talk.

Do not let your past unhappiness – or fear of the future – destroy your present contentment. We try to control our lives, needing certainty, but we cannot. Thoughts are not facts. We have a choice in how we feel. We can always choose how we respond.

A Mindful approach to forgiveness

"Holding on to resentment is like drinking poison hoping the other person will die." Anon.

Forgiveness is not about condoning, pardoning, forgetting or letting someone off the hook: we can maintain that the behaviour was unacceptable, while lessening our own emotional burdens and healing the pain of our heart by first remembering, telling our story and validating our feelings.

Forgiveness is a process that happens over time and it is about accepting responsibility for our emotional reactions. We decide to see a situation differently, using wisdom and compassion rather than instinctive 'negative' emotions. It is a 'weakness' in another that drove them to act the way they did. If we are holding on to hurt, we remember that we can decide what we do with it.

Eventually, forgiveness releases us from the burden of pain and anger. It does not mean blindly trusting someone who has let us down: we can forgive someone and never trust them again. How do you want to be defined and to define yourself? You don't want to be described as a victim; by letting go of anger and resentment you are taking personal responsibility and rejecting the role of the victim so that you can take back your power.

Forgiveness involves surrendering your right to punish, to get even. It results in freedom from emotional pain and the hold the other person has over you. The Buddha taught that if we do not forgive, we keep creating an identity around our pain so that it keeps being reborn and causing us further suffering. Dwelling on bitterness and anger consumes us, not another person. The main cause of suffering is the yo-yo of 'grasping and aversion' that we human beings go through. According to Ghandi, forgiveness is an attribute that strong people have.

Forgiveness is said to improve mental and physical health and assist psychological healing and wellbeing. However, a forced form of 'forgiving' may be the worst thing you can do, if you are doing it because people say you must. Do not fixate on the hurt as fixating leaves you frozen. We must take baby steps, accepting that how we feel is how we feel – at the same time realising that we must stop identifying with the suffering we were caused, being more than a victim of our past. Accepting what has happened is not to condone it, either. It just means that *it has happened*. That was then and this, now, is the present. Having the desire to forgive, but struggling and 'failing' can lead to resenting and blaming and not feeling spiritual, so take your time and use regular Mindfulness exercises: develop resilience.

My precious teacher, Akong Rinpoche, was murdered on 8th October 2013. His brother, Lama Yeshe Rinpoche immediately forgave his killers and gave a moving tribute to Rinpoche at Samye Ling exactly a year later, commencing with "I am a very happy man. I am happy because I live completely in the present." Rinpoche would never have wanted us to be hateful or angry towards his killers. Instead, he would want his students to carry on his legacy, helping others – which is what many of us are doing.

Thinking of forgiveness when we are suffering, we may be inclined to say "They do not deserve forgiveness." or "Why would I ever be able to forgive someone who has treated me so badly?" And then there is self-forgiveness: so many of us ignore the fact that we carry around a huge festering ball of lack of forgiveness for ourselves. Forgiveness is a process and we do not have to combat our own resistance but simply go with the flow. Forgiving ourselves for being duped is very important – seeing the positive aspects of being *forced* to be in a loving relationship with ourselves. See **Exercise 13**.

It may also be fair to say that someone who accepts no accountability for what they have done and has no remorse may be very difficult to forgive. One woman said "I can't forgive a crime that is 'still in progress'!" Forgiveness is, in some ways, the opposite of holding on to resentment. So the best way

I have found to look at it is to decide to be more than a victim of my past and move on, forgiving the situation that I was in, forgiving myself for being so 'stupid', not condoning the ex, but forgiving the part of him that meant he suffers so much that the only way for him to live is to feed off others. So we can pity that side of people who abuse us, for sure, even if we can't 'forgive' immediately – that can come later.

Think of it this way: If you ask 'What is my motivation?' before you do anything, you can keep yourself on the straight and narrow. If your motivation is revenge or to harm another, DO NOT GO THERE. What is the point in accumulating bad karma for yourself? Let BE. Let the Universe sort it out for you. What goes around comes around, eventually.

One wise woman I met advised: "Forgive and Forget!" She went on to say: "Forgive him for being a selfish fool and forget that he exists!" I found that amusing and very helpful in dissolving anger!

Rebuilding and self-love

"Your task is not to seek for Love, but merely to seek and find all the barriers within yourself that you have built against it." Rumi·

Recovering from heartbreak involves a journey to self-love. Self-love is *not* selfish and involves self-forgiveness. It is a difficult task but it is important to rid ourselves of the emotional imperative to have a partner. Despondency can emerge when we think about all the times we have 'failed'. When we talk about 'failed' relationships we forget that we have all had many relationships and by definition, no longer being in them, the very large majority of the others didn't 'work' because we are no longer together!

We are not always very logical with our self-talk. Those who do not know how to love themselves can be plagued with self-doubt which can lead to unhappiness, even depression and self-hatred. You may have thought that everything that went wrong was your fault and you were unlovable so you can put yourself down. You may have hidden yourself away but your 'protection' can lead to disempowerment. Do not give away your strength.

Take it one day at a time and use your breath to stay in the present – using 3 deep Mindful breaths (**Exercise 4**) and observe when you keep slipping into the past or rushing into the future. It is fascinating how we can be intelligent people but still keep going back to the past, somehow 'believing' on one level, that we can change something: over and over again with frightening regularity. By practising radical acceptance of 'what is' we can allow the feelings to come and go like a wave remembering that nothing (good or bad) stays the same.

It is important to cut the etheric connections that exist between us and others when the relationship has ended. If we are unaware of an unbroken cord between us and another person, emotions and energy continue to flow between us, keeping the connection alive. See **Exercise 10**.

We have tricky brains and we can over-react because of the ancient survival programme of 'fight or flight'. So many people worry about what other people think of them. I have seen this in a lot of young women and I find CBT useful. See **Exercise 23**. Most of us are far too busy getting on with our lives and simply do not have the time to be judging others.

What is important is our opinion of our self. That self really deserves our kindness, our compassion, our forgiveness for not being perfect. What sort of 'internal person' do you want to be spending time with: someone who constantly gives you a hard time and puts you down or someone who cherishes you?

Life is short. Life is precious. If we thought really logically we would not want to waste the precious seconds, minutes, hours of our lives putting ourselves down. We are so often our biggest critic. Living in our own authentic presence is so much more fulfilling. There comes a time in our lives when we have to realise that whatever we have done or said cannot be changed. All we can do is to move forward with forgiveness and respect for ourselves. It is freeing. See **Exercise 14**.

When we mindfully observe what is happening in the present moment the old stale stuff can drop away. We learn to ask ourselves what we want and cherish ourselves and our uniqueness.

In my workshops I tell people that the most important person in their life is themselves. When I recently told a student I was in a loving relationship with myself, she completely misunderstood what I was saying and exclaimed "Oh, that is so sad!"; illustrating that she believed I was either so embittered I wasn't going to care for others any more, or that I had turned into a very selfish person! What I *actually* meant was that after years of putting myself down and not caring for myself I had finally learned to turn the love and attention I was putting out to others towards myself, with an attitude of kindness and compassion.

When you are genuinely in such a relationship with yourself, you can come across to others as more contented and kind, loving and generous. I enjoy life by myself and with others and I do not feel the loneliness I felt when I was in an unhappy relationship. I still have me and I am so grateful and happy for that. There is also confusion between self-love and narcissism. The difference in those states is that whereas self-love is healthy, narcissism means using others to serve you. Practising self-love means being gentle, kind and accepting to yourself *and* others.

At the same time, challenging mind-states like anxiety, depression or anger can pop up and frighten us unexpectedly during our recovery and we might consider taking medical advice, even short-term herbal medicine or allopathic medicine. We can use Mindfulness and when we pay heed to Rumi's poem The Guest House (**Exercise 9**) we can invite those visitors in, welcoming them and being grateful for what they are telling us.

We are told to 'be positive'. Indeed, Akong Rinpoche, told me to 'turn negative into positive'. By that, he did not mean to ignore what was, because he also told me to 'be Mindful all day every day' which means not practising suppression but rather its opposite: acceptance. It is not the fatalistic acceptance of a status quo but acceptance of 'what is' so that it can be healed. We learn to be kind and compassionate to ourselves. **Exercise 13** is helpful.

The reality check-list

What did you learn from the relationship that enabled you to grow?

What feelings are you holding on to that you need to release?

What did you lose in the relationship? What did you find?

What was your worst, most painful moment?

What things did the other person say that upset you?

Were you brainwashed or manipulated?

Were you under a spell?

When the spell breaks, you finally gain insight and self-acceptance and the ability to be in a loving relationship with yourself

SECTION FIVE

RECOVERY STEPS – THE JOURNEY BACK TO YOURSELF

"Only say nice things about people. Don't be angry. Don't be jealous. Be careful what you say. Bring people together. Talk about good things. If you cannot, close your mouth: chatter is a waste of time. Try to do good every day. First, train your mind. Do not try to do charity work in the beginning. Once your mind is trained, all your actions become charity. Try to live your life on the basis of Buddhist principles."

Akong Rinpoche, teaching in the Temple at Samye Ling, 2006

The journey of recovery after heartbreak takes time and has many steps:

Negative self-talk

Fear of being unworthy

Heightened fear of abandonment

Guilt, shame and self-blame

I 'should' be back to normal

Bad attitude and lack of self-care

Some days you will not want to get out of bed

Not showering, dressing or brushing your teeth

Withdrawing from others

Perpetually in fight or flight mode

If you have low self esteem you might overlook the signs that things aren't right

You may have lost touch with friends and family

Beware social phobia

When in a trough of despond:

Be aware that you may have been bewitched and beguiled

Understand HOW you were exploited

Beware of false accusations from your ex-partner and their taking the moral high ground so you blame yourself and give in to regrets

Remember, you are connected to everything and you are loved and safe

Slowly, slowly you recover from betrayal, abandonment and indifference

Remember, your primary relationship is with yourself

Rid yourself of dependency on others and their opinions of you

Listen to your heart-mind and gut-mind as well as your brain-mind

Remember that sometimes a part of us must die before another part comes to life

Discover your strengths

Positively, the experience can lead to change in the way you live – with new strengths, new patterns, new optimism and the ability to help others

Eventually you will emerge: your life-path has changed for the better

Remember, a toxic relationship can be a bottomless pit of need

Everyone has their own path

Don't push emotions/feelings away: what we resist persists

Do not give in to denial – acknowledge what is happening. Sit with it. Surrender

Accept the pain, the fear, the hurt

We cannot choose the way someone behaves, but we can choose our reaction to them

Be aware

Recovery may be a long process of putting one foot in front of the other

You can suffer from a non-descript anxiety

Chronic unhappiness leads to despair and depression.

Obsessing about the past prevents your ability to be happy

One of the biggest fears of survivors of emotional abuse, is that their former partner will be happy with someone else and THEY will be alone and unhappy – life is NEVER that black and white

Working towards recovery

Reach acceptance of the end

Be detached and watch what is going on within yourself

Listen to your intuition, or 'inner tuition'

Identify fears and limiting beliefs

Remember that you cannot be happy if you are held back by the past

Remember you cannot change that past

Honour your own feelings and suffering first and practice loving-kindness to yourself

You must 'do the time' recovery-wise

Know that life is a series of ups and downs and that nothing stays the same

Be careful

Be choosey who you talk to about your recovery

Avoid people who tell you, in so many words, to pull yourself together and just get over it

Choose carefully who you work with: many professionals do not understand toxic relationships

Set boundaries so you do not over-stretch yourself

Protect yourself from psychic vampires

Question whether you have forgiven yourself and whether you are blaming yourself

If you believe in soul lessons, remember that holding on to a grudge is a colossal waste of time

Remind yourself

When we have been in a toxic relationship, regardless of the suffering we have been through, the lesson we learn is that we are actually capable of loving

In the future, run from toxic people

Sometimes we must get away from someone for our own good

Honour your experience as you would an important teacher

You are stronger than you think

You have handled what life has thrown at you

You will recover and you have learnt lessons

Repeat "I am enough"

Anger can fuel change – it is simply a mind-state

You will not be punished *for* your anger: you will be punished *by* your anger

You must embrace, not bypass, the pain otherwise you set yourself up to fail

Compassion, empathy and love are not weaknesses

Do not become isolated – do things which ensure you meet people and consider helping others

Cultivate an attitude of gratitude for small things

Practise radical acceptance

Give the love you have to give to yourself first

Recognise that feelings are just feelings and allow them to arise, show themselves and dissolve

Know that true recovery involves finding the courage to face your deepest fears

Accept that the healing process can be challenging

Painful memories are suddenly triggered like fish popping up in a pond, leaving ripples which soon disappear

Anger is just a mind-state

Positive thinking

Remember, when you are stuck in the trough of despond, cracks allow the light in

Live with intentionality – in other words, be in the driving seat of your life

Appreciate your *own* feelings of love that you had during the relationship

Practise kindness towards yourself

Keep going

Refuse to be a victim

Forgive the person for their constitutional inability to stay constant in love

Concentrate on the good things in your life

Check in with what your needs are

Develop healthy interactions with people

Learn to understand what is someone else's issue – this will help you to move on and not be bitter

Actively doing

Keep paper and pen available so that you can 'vomit on the page' any thoughts that arise

List what you want to do on your bucket list

Meditate on a daily basis

Write in a 'thoughts journal'

Actively practise Mindfulness to slowly face and tolerate the painful feelings and slow down the afflictive and repetitive thought patterns

Use "How curious" to take the sting out of the situation, as in "How curious this thought is popping up again"

Come back to your breath and body in an intentional way throughout the day

Looking after your mind

Avoid too much social media, especially 'Stalkbook'

Remember that every emotion is temporary – nothing stays the same

Distract yourself with small pleasures

Set boundaries

Cultivate your spiritual practice

Forgive yourself and practice self-compassion

Forgive others and practice compassion for them

Trust yourself and your inner tuition (gut/heart minds)

Feel whole, complete and content just being with yourself

Work with a counsellor, psychologist, coach or anyone recommended to you to help

Be curious about destructive cravings

Remember, Mindfulness engages the rational side of the brain, helping you to move forward with intention.

Accept that Mindfulness helps us to learn from our mistakes

Be grateful for your freedom to be yourself

Surround yourself with support offered by friends and family

Be gentle with yourself

Join a forum/self-help group

Learn from the past – gaining perspective allows you to be poised and not poisoned

Repeat "I deserve to receive happiness in abundance and love"

Change your routine and do different things

Read self-empowering books

Watch DVDs that make you laugh

Write down what is troubling you to rid your mind of it

Looking after mind/body

How about embracing your anger in a constructive way such as taking up boxing or kick boxing, or body combat classes at the gym?

Decide to rearrange your home, if you lived there with your ex: it is hard to stay in the same place as the 'scene of the crime'

Looking after your body

Eat a balanced diet

Exercise regularly

Walk often

If you do not have a dog to walk, consider walking a neighbour's or one from the dogs' home

Have massage, reflexology and healing

Avoid mindless self-medication with alcohol and drugs

Light a candle, perform a ritual for recovery

Use essential oils such as lavender and clary sage

Use relaxation techniques

Sleep well (Use **Exercise 11** – scanning the body – to help you sleep)

Eat well and use vitamin supplements

Take Mindful breaks during the day with Mindful breathing and being in nature.

Really commune with nature

Mindfully watch and listen to birds

Mindfully breathe in healing throughout the day

Mindfully watch comedies

Drink a lot of water

SECTION SIX

EXERCISES FOR MINDFUL
SELF-COMPASSIONATE LIVING

"Be Mindful of what you do: talking, eating, actions ... that way everything becomes spiritual. Something is not spiritual unless your MIND is in it. Mindfulness concerns thinking, talking and moving. If you are Mindful all the time you are spiritual all the time. If you are Mindful you do not cause suffering. Regular Mindfulness is very useful for developing a positive mind. Everyone is human and we all make mistakes."

Akong Rinpoche, teaching in the Temple at Samye Ling

ABOUT THE EXERCISES AND RECOMMENDED APPROACH

These exercises are relatively short and simply explained so that people are more likely to use them. Many of them can be practised absolutely anywhere. The important thing to remember is that ANY form of Mindfulness practice will bring you great benefit; and the more you practise, the more you will bring beneficial changes into your life.

For EVERY practice, including walking practices, keep a pad of paper and pencil close to you. That way, if a thought arises that you find yourself trying to hold on to, you can jot it onto the pad and return to 'being on the spot'. It also helps to have tissues and a glass of water handy, too.

You may wish to make friends with a pebble or two – they can be very useful for focus. Some people like to look down their noses at them but most of my students like to have them sitting in the palm of their upturned hand.

Finally, practising Mindfulness is about BEING, not doing. Have an open, child-like approach and do not strive to 'get it right'. Accept that you are where you are – even if your life feels like a mess – do not resist what arises but allow it to arise, display and dissolve. Everything takes its own time so honour your own feelings and trust yourself.

LIST OF MINDFULNESS EXERCISES

1. Sitting by the stream
2. A basic Mindfulness sitting practice
3. 5-minute Mindfulness practice
4. 3 deep Mindful breaths
5. Breathing in a healing colour to the whole of your body
6. Being with your pebble
7. Day-breaks
8. Embracing the inevitable: experiencing true acceptance
9. The Guest House and RAIN
10. Mindfully cutting the chords that tie you to another person
11. Scanning your body
12. Breathing in soft pink light to your heart
13. Letting be through forgiveness of yourself, with self-compassion
14. Being 100 – contemplating impermanence
15. Taking back the pieces of your heart
16. Clearing/ripping/burning
17. Mindful walking
18. Sitting with water
19. Being with a tree/contemplating nature or a garden
20. What do I want?
21. Visualising a place of wellness
22. Mindfully listening to music
23. Actively dealing with self-criticism
24. Use of triggers
25. Knowing yourself
26. Sitting with your morning coffee

EXERCISE 1 – Sitting by the stream

We can imagine that our life is like a stream. From small beginnings, it starts to flow, twists and turns and has various additions along the way, increasing and decreasing in volume until it eventually joins the ocean. Does the stream carry debris or does it flow freely?

Equally, there is a stream of thoughts that constantly flows, day and night, 24-hours a day, through our brain-mind. It can flow quietly and gently or it can flow as a noisy torrent depending on what is happening in our lives. We learn to Mindfully deal with 'what is', even if we feel we are sitting in a puddle of despair!

We are the watcher of this stream. When we start to realise that this is happening and we can in some way distance ourselves from identifying with the stream and allow ourselves just to BE and watch the stream, our life becomes more workable. It is our natural inclination to aspire to having positive thoughts, while the reality is that because we are human when we become aware of our thoughts they are often connected to problem-solving and thus by definition more 'negative'.

In order to help us to deal with what is occurring in the stream of our crazy mind, we can learn just to witness what is happening without becoming too engaged. A Tibetan Buddhist expression I love is 'Not too tight, nor too loose' – so finding the 'sweet spot' in our mind where we allow thoughts to arise without overly-engaging our neuroses is important.

Sit on a cushion or chair and breathe into your stomach area. Either look down your nose at a fixed spot – or even a real stream if you are out in nature – or close your eyes.

First, ensure that you are sitting comfortably and will be able to remain relaxed in that position for the next 5 or 10 minutes or longer.

Now, be aware of your body and any areas of discomfort. Make little adjustments to your position, if necessary and breathe into any areas of discomfort. Now tell yourself 'I can be aware of the flowing stream of my thoughts' and, as if you are watching a television screen, watch what appears there.

Just allow. Just be. Your thoughts may manifest themselves as self-talk; in which case, listen to that self-talk. So allow your thoughts to arise and show themselves to you, then watch them join the stream of your mind.

Do not suppress any thoughts. Thoughts are not good or bad, they are just 'thinking'. If something arises that alarms you, simply say 'How curious': "How curious that I am thinking that again." "How curious that this keeps coming up." The more you sit and watch the stream, the easier it will be for you to recognise that YOU ARE NOT YOUR THOUGHTS.

Use your breath as an anchor to come back to every time you find you have leapt into the stream to follow a thought!

By practising Mindfulness we can learn to slowly tolerate and face any painful feelings and slow down the afflictive and repetitive thought patterns.

We cannot avoid suffering – we can choose to view change as an avenue to personal evolution.

EXERCISE 2 - A basic Mindfulness sitting practice

Give yourself time to arrive on your chair or cushion, with anything you might need to hand (pad, pencil, water, tissues) Make any adjustments necessary to ensure you will be comfortable – do not just sit rigidly immediately and hold the position because you think that is what you are supposed to do. Have a relaxed and careful attitude. Have the right temperature for you (open a window if you are hot, have a warm wrap around you if you are cold).

If sitting on a chair, be aware of your feet on the floor. Be aware of your sitting bones on the surface on which they are resting. Your back has natural curves so obey those curves as you sit – do not hold your back like a poker, rather sit alert and awake and yet relaxed.

Shrug your shoulders up to your ears then move them back and down, at the same time as you drop your hands, one on top of the other, palms up into your lap.

This allows for opening in the chest and stomach area.

The back of your neck is long – retract your chin slightly to allow lengthening.

Imagine a golden thread descending from the sky, attaching itself to the top of your head and giving you a little tug, so that there is alignment, back of the head, back of the neck and back.

You are aware of being 'on the spot' – with nowhere else to go and nothing else to do. Be aware of the solidity of your body. We live in a world surrounded by sounds: sounds from outside the room in which you are, inside the room and maybe even inside your body. If out in nature, be aware of all of the sounds – distant and nearby. Just allow all of those sounds to knit together like one big blanket of sound that hovers over you, hearing them without actively listening, so that any further sounds that arise simply join the generic comfort blanket of sound.

Breathing in and breathing out – place your attention on the area between your neck and your groin – be aware of your chest and stomach area: breathing all the way in to your stomach, with expansion and all the way out with contraction. Continue to do this throughout the meditation.

Allow your thoughts to arise and dissolve into the stream without clinging to them. Thoughts are not good or bad; they are just thinking. You are the watcher of the stream.

With Mindfulness there are 3 main supports: sound, breath, pebble. With the pebble, we either place it in front of us so that we can look down our nose at it or on the palm of our hand so that we are aware of the *feel* of the pebble on our hand (a kinaesthetic anchor). We can use all 3 supports or just one.

These supports are used as an anchor, in the following way: Imagine, if you will, a little rowing boat just close to the sea shore. The anchor has been thrown overboard and is resting on the sea bed. The little boat is drifting here and there, according to the winds and waves until the rope connecting the anchor to the boat grows taut and tugs at the boat, which gently drifts back to the anchor. And so it is with your chosen support, as your anchor. When you observe that you are following your thoughts instead of allowing them to arise, display and dissolve, gently return to your chosen support, again and again.

Breathing in, breathing out, expansion, contraction, rise and fall. Just be. And return, gently, again and again to your support. Thoughts are just thoughts. Observe them as they join the stream in your brain-mind. Thoughts, emotions, sensations and images are free to arise and to dissolve as the stream flows.

Continue for 5, 10, 15 minutes – however long you have allowed yourself. The important thing is that you endeavour to practise regularly. Come back to where you are, slowly and gently.

EXERCISE 3 – 5-minute Mindfulness practice

Imagine an hourglass – wide at the top, narrow in the middle and wide at the bottom.

Sit comfortably, then be aware of how you are feeling, of any sounds surrounding you, of breathing in and out, of any thoughts that are in the stream of your mind – allowing them to just BE. Quickly scan the whole of your body and breathe into any discomfort you might be feeling. Remember to keep your back upright and aligned with your head and back of the neck but not rigid.

Now place your attention on the area between your neck and your groin and watch your chest and stomach area expand and contract as you breathe all the way in to your stomach and all the way out again. Say in your head 'breathing in, breathing out' slowly and deliberately as you do it. Get into a slow rhythm.

After a couple of minutes, place your attention once again on the whole of your body, watching it move as you breathe, the rise and fall of your breath and body. Be aware of your facial expression and how you feel. After a few more breaths, come back very slowly to where you are.

EXERCISE 4 – 3 deep Mindful breaths

This practice is short and sweet and can be done any time any place anywhere. I call it the 'toilet meditation' so that people remember it, and remember to do it when they visit what we Brits call 'the loo'.

Whether you are sitting, standing or lying, place your single-pointed attention on the area between your neck and your groin.

Slowly and deliberately breathe in to your stomach area, making it expand and saying during the *whole* time of the breath 'Now I am breathing in'. As you breathe out, allowing your tummy to contract, and during the whole time of the breath, say 'Now I am breathing out'. Remember to keep your focus on your chest and tummy and concentrate on really *feeling* the words as you say them very deliberately.

Do this three times. Your eyes can be open or shut, depending on where you are. Then come back to where you are. If you are enjoying yourself you can, of course, continue!

EXERCISE 5 – Breathing in a healing colour to the whole of your body

This short practice is best done sitting or lying down. It can be done like exercise 4 (3 deep Mindful breaths) or you can continue for as long as you like. It is inspired by the work of my precious teacher, Akong Rinpoche and his book 'Taming the Tiger'.

Choose a colour that represents healing and cleansing to you.

Then, placing your attention on the area between your neck and your groin, deliberately, as you breathe in to your chest and abdomen, imagine the colour entering you, rushing to every cell in your body.

Then, as you breathe all the way out, imagine that at the same time you are breathing out dark grey smoke of stale energy that dissolves as it leaves your body.

Repeat this exercise for as long as you wish.

EXERCISE 6 – Being with your pebble

In Mindfulness, the three main supports that we use are sound, breath and a pebble. Many students become attached to their pebble(s). Some use a small one that they place in a pocket so that every time they feel it they are reminded to be Mindful.

Place your pebble in front of you so that you can look down your nose at it while you are sitting in a meditation position. Just allow your gaze to rest upon the pebble. You do not have to do anything else. By being 'on the spot' you may begin to see what thoughts are arising.

Keep coming back to breathing in and out with your gaze still placed on the pebble.

Do this for as long as you like. Even 60 seconds several times a day will make a difference to your life.

EXERCISE 7 – Day-breaks

Schedule breaks to check-in with yourself by monitoring your breathing and thoughts. This will prevent a full-blown downward spiral if you are being plagued with negative thinking.

Sitting, lying, standing or walking, quickly scan your body and how it feels. Then look at your brain-mind – how are you?

Whatever comes up, remember that thoughts are just thinking and allow yourself the tiny amount of space and time necessary to breathe very deeply into your stomach area, smiling to yourself as you do, then breathe slowly out again. That is all!

EXERCISE 8 – Embracing the inevitable: experiencing true acceptance

This poignant and powerful exercise is inspired by Tara Brach's inspirational book 'Radical Acceptance' and in particular her exercise on p.87: 'The power of Yes'.

Our natural inclination, when facing heartbreak, is to suppress the feelings, to bottle things up, to the point of denial. For this exercise, it is important that you are alone and will not be disturbed.

Bring your Mindfulness journal and a pen, a glass of water and a box of tissues to your usual chair and place them beside you where you can reach them. Sitting comfortably, go through the short Mindfulness practice of settling yourself, feeling grounded and deciding on the support or supports you will use. Find the stillness within yourself. Breathe into your stomach area.

Bring to mind the emotional situation of heartbreak in which you find yourself. Really *feel* what is going on, in your body as well as your brain-mind. Take your time.

Then direct 'No' to the situation. No to what has happened. No to the loss. No to the heartbreak. No to all of the emotions you are feeling. No. No. No. Keep saying No and as you do, feel what is happening for you – what effect is this refusal having on you, your body, your mind, your emotions?

Then ask yourself "How will I *be* in 3 days, 3 weeks, 3 months and 3 years if I continue to say 'No', if I continue to *refuse* to accept what has happened?" Write down what comes to mind.

Get up, shake your body, take some deep breaths and then, again, sit comfortably, finding the stillness, breathing into your tummy. Again, bring to mind the situation, really *feeling* it.

Now direct a very deliberate and gentle 'Yes' to the situation. Yes to the heartbreak and loss, yes to the pain. Yes. Yes. Yes. This part can be very emotional. Do not hold on to any feelings – if you need to cry tears or cry out, do so. And remember to be *gentle* with yourself.

Then, still with 'Yes' in your mind, ask yourself "How will I *be* in 3 days, 3 weeks, 3 months and 3 years if I continue to say 'Yes', if I continue to *accept* what has happened in a whole-hearted way?"

Write down anything that comes to mind. Sit with your feelings. Allow any waves of emotion to gently wash over you.

You will experience the positive power of acceptance by doing this exercise. It may be painful, you may encounter resistance within yourself and yet you will begin to realise that by embracing 'what is' rather than continually ruminating over the past you can give yourself permission to stop clinging to a past you cannot change, and move forward – one foot in front of the other. You will see the sense of accepting what is there anyway. It is liberating.

EXERCISE 9 – The Guest House and RAIN*

*You awake, and for one tenth of a second you feel fine. Then your heart sinks and you remember why you do not; or you are suddenly overtaken by an emotion you just cannot shift; or you simply find yourself stuck in painful rumination. All of these situations and many, many more call for the use of this exercise where you face your fears rather than suppress them. Reading this poem is the first step, followed by the use of '**RAIN**':*

The Guest House
This being human is a guest house.
Every morning a new arrival.
A joy, a depression, a meanness,
some momentary awareness comes
as an unexpected visitor.

Welcome and entertain them all!
Even if they are a crowd of sorrows
who violently sweep your house
empty of its furniture,
still, treat each guest honorably.
He may be clearing you out
for some new delight.

The dark thought, the shame, the malice,
meet them at the door laughing,

and invite them in.
Be grateful for whoever comes,
because each has been sent
as a guide from beyond.

∞

Always check your inner state
with the lord of your heart.
Copper doesn't know it's copper,
until it's changing to gold.
Your loving doesn't know majesty,
until it knows its helplessness.

(1st 3 verses: The Guest House, Essential Rumi p.109; the 4th verse from The Mouse and the Camel in This Longing, pp. 32-33. Translated by Coleman Barks and used with his kind permission)

Settle yourself where you are and breathe deeply into your stomach area. With this beautiful poetry in mind, pay attention to the difficult thought or emotion that is knocking at the door of your guest house. Use RAIN to address it:

Step 1– Recognise: Recognise what the emotion or feeling is and name it. This is like opening the door and acknowledging the guest that wants to enter your metaphorical or imagined guest house.

Step 2 – Allow: Next, simply allow the emotion or feeling to be present. This is like welcoming the guest and inviting it to take a seat inside your guest house.

Step 3 – Inquire/Investigate: Ask yourself where in your body you are holding the guest. Notice what sensations are going on in your body. Then examine what stories are present for you with regards to the unwelcome guest. Is it one emotion or a kaleidoscope of emotions? Is it new or a frequent visitor? Does it have a message for you? Finally, are you taking the emotion to be solid and are you identifying with it as who you are? Be kind to yourself.

Step 4 – Non-identify

This leads to the last stage of RAIN, in which you ask yourself: "Is this state who I am, or is it simply passing through me?" There is only one possible answer – "It is not me, it is simply [name it] passing through me." Allow yourself to fully feel what is going on. At the same time, you can feel and say "This too will pass" – the guest will eventually leave the guest house – "So I can get on with the rest of my day and leave it sitting in my guest house until it gets up and leaves, shutting the door behind it."

*Michele McDonald was the first person to use the acronym RAIN.

EXERCISE 10 – Mindfully cutting the chords that tie you to another person

You have love to receive and share and so much to live for although you cannot see it yet, but in order to see it you must let go of the past – because hanging on to it can be an addiction that hurts you more. Where is the grief/anger/emotional pain being held in your body? It is often held in the liver area. Do something to let it go. For the sake of your life-yet-to-be you need to let go of holding on and move on, reclaiming yourself, using your sword of truth to visualise yourself cutting the ties.

Sit on a chair or on the floor. If on a chair, place another chair in front of you. If on the floor, place a cushion or other object in front of you to represent the other. Place a lit candle between you and the other seat. Summon up the awareness that cutting chords with someone can separate you from unnecessary and unhelpful attachments. It is freeing. Settle well into your sitting position, allow your body to relax and start breathing deeply into your stomach area.

Call to mind the person and the situation that you wish to let BE – in other words you bring it all to mind and instead of pushing it away, decide that you are going to cut any chords that are attaching you to the other person and visualise where these chords might be attached to you (your heart? solar plexus? stomach?).

Tell them what you think of the situation and why you wish to let them be in their own space away from you, and then imagine taking your 'sword of truth' (which can be as beautiful and jewel-encrusted as you wish) and slice through the invisible chords, imagining that any 'wounds' you may have are filled with healing light and heal over so that the energetic chords cannot enter you again. See all of the attachments shrivelling away from you, dissolving, disappearing.

When you feel that you are done, surround yourself with a bubble of white light and imagine the other person encased in a similar bubble of white light and then watch them gently float away from you. There is nothing that binds you together any more.

If you are very attached to the person or find yourself ruminating very strongly, you can repeat the exercise as many times as you need. It helps to bathe in Epsom salts and 5 drops of essential oil of lavender afterwards.

EXERCISE 11 – Scanning your body

This exercise is very useful for relaxation and helps people to drift off to sleep when they are tense (in fact I refer to it as 'boring yourself to sleep'). It can be done sitting, even standing but is best done lying down. Do this exercise at a slow and rhythmic pace.

Get yourself warm and comfortable. Be aware of your body and the way that you are holding yourself. Breathe into any areas of tension or discomfort. Be aware of the rise and fall of your breath as you breathe all the way in to your stomach area, and all the way out again, with expansion and contraction.

Then place your attention on to your 2 big toes. How do they feel? Then all of your toes... the top of your feet... the soles of your feet... your heels... all 4 ankle bones... your shins... your calves... the front and back of your knees... the front of your thighs... the back of your thighs... your hips... your sitting bones... your groin... your lower back... your stomach... your upper back... your chest... your shoulders.

Jackie Hawken

Place your attention on your 2 thumbs... then all of
your fingers... the back of your hands... the palm of
your hands... your wrists... the front of your lower
arms... the back of your lower arms... your elbows...
the front of your upper arms... the back of your upper
arms... your armpits.

Place your attention on your throat... the back of your
neck... your chin... your mouth... your nose... your
ears... your eyes... your forehead... the back of your
head... the crown of your head...

And then go back down slightly quicker: the crown of
your head... the back of your head... your forehead...
your eyes... your ears... your nose... your mouth...
your chin... the back of your neck... your throat... your
armpits... the back of your upper arms... the front of
your upper arms... your elbow... the back of your
lower arms... the front of your lower arms... your
wrists... the palm of your hands... the back of your
hands... all of your fingers... your 2 thumbs... your

146

shoulders... your chest... your upper back... your stomach... your lower back... your groin... your sitting bones... your hips... the back of your thighs... the front of your thighs... the front and back of your knees... your calves... your shins... all 4 ankle bones... your heels... the soles of your feet... the top of your feet... all of your toes... your big toes.

Then be aware again of the whole of your body and your breath as you breathe into your stomach area. Have awareness of the expression on your face. Slowly move your body and notice how you are: of course, you may have fallen asleep before you get to this point!

EXERCISE 12 – Breathing in soft pink light to your heart

The vulnerable, open, honest way in which you learn to see, name and look everything in the eye is part of your healing. You do not suppress the pain but feel it so that you can feel whole again and move on. If you are able to cry it will help to flush out your feelings.

Find a comfortable position with an open chest, heart and stomach area. Be aware of any painful feelings that you may have. Allow them to rise to the surface.

Then think of a soft pink light and *s l o w l y* breathe all the way in, imagining the light entering your heart. Breathe *s l o w l y* all the way out, imagining that you are breathing out all the pain and uncomfortable feelings connected to your suffering.

Ride the waves of your feelings with your breath. Do this at least 3 times but continue for longer if you have time.

EXERCISE 13 – Letting be through forgiveness for yourself, with self-compassion

Don't blame yourself for things that have happened in the past. You need to give yourself permission to eventually have an honest and stable relationship with yourself and then with others. Create space in your life, first to heal and then to look forward.

Sit on a chair or cushion, taking time to relax and ensure that you are comfortable. Your back is upright, obeying the natural curves and your hands are in your lap. Breathe slowly in and out to your stomach area, allow any thoughts to arise, display and dissolve into the stream of your mind.

Remind yourself of what stories you are holding onto.

Now feel the breath going into your heart and tell yourself that you create heartache when you do not forgive yourself. Now remind yourself that you deserve your own compassion and forgiveness. Allow troubling thoughts which you are holding on to, to arise. Watch them, do not internalise them.

Keep repeating to yourself in your head, as you slowly breathe in and out to your stomach area:

"I forgive myself. I love myself. I deserve my compassion. I deserve all good things"

Feel a softening in your heart and body as you do this. Do this for at least 10 deep breaths in and out.

You can also use this exercise to forgive others, when you feel that you are strong enough and that you have managed to forgive yourself first. Often we feel angry and unforgiving towards others because we are angry towards ourselves for what we have allowed to happen.

EXERCISE 14 – Being 100 – contemplating impermanence

This exercise is very useful when you have spiralled out of control – it helps to concentrate your mind and realise what a waste it is to give energy to negative situations

Have a pad and pen with you. Adopt a seated position with a comfortable back and breathe all the way in to your stomach area, all the way out again for a few breaths. Then say to yourself:

-   I am now 100 years old
-   Looking back on my life, what do I wish I had done less of?
-   What do I wish I had done more of?

Really concentrate on the 2 questions. In particular, think of the energy and time that is spent on being angry, resentful, hateful or ruminating over situations. And think of what you could have spent the time doing instead. Really *feel* the loss of time spent on useless emotions. And then remember – you are not

100! You are fortunate! You have time! Do not waste it.

Write down what comes up, as a reminder. Do this exercise as often as you need to.

EXERCISE 15 – Taking back the pieces of your heart

Go for a walk in nature. Breathe in deeply as you walk. Look up and out. Be very present.

Call to mind the heartbreak situation that you are dealing with. Be aware of how you are feeling, particularly with regard to the person that you used to be in a relationship with and how they have not looked after the pieces of your heart that they still have.

Repeat many times until you feel you are calm and have made a difference to yourself:

"I take back to me all that is mine, every piece of my heart. I give back to you everything of yours I may have. "

Really *feel* that your heart is becoming whole.

Repeat this exercise on a daily basis. It is very cathartic.

EXERCISE 16 – Clearing/ripping/burning

Be aware of holding on to momentos from your past relationship. When the time is right, take everything you have that you are able to let go of – clearing your home of what needs to go to rid yourself of the illusion that you were under. Then rip up what you can and take everything out into your garden, or in nature, and set fire to it.

Be present as this is happening. Be Mindful and in the present moment and most importantly – be kind to yourself. Know that it takes time to rid yourself of the rumination over the past relationship. Depending on the nature and the length of the relationship it can take several years.

Follow this with some form of ceremonial space-clearing in your home – you could use salt in every corner of every room that you clean up after 24 hours, or use sound in every corner of every room, or waft joss-sticks around. Whatever you use, concentrate on new beginnings and letting stale energy dissipate.

If you can, go for a Mindful walk (**Exercise 17**) afterwards.

EXERCISE 17 – Mindful walking

When out for a walk, whether in an urban or a rural environment, for five minutes or for an hour, you can walk Mindfully.

Mindful walking involves paying attention to your environment and your body. Go outside for a walk with the real intention of being fully in the present moment:

Ask yourself, taking adequate time to observe and *feel* it:

What can I see?

What can I hear?

What can I smell?

Is there a taste in my mouth?

What can I touch?

How do I feel?

How do my feet feel as I move them, one foot after the other?

Every time you find that your mind has drifted back to the usual chatter (often problem-solving, which is a habit many of us have developed over the years when we are out walking) ask yourself the same questions again – and again...

Be present, be observant and enjoy the moment. This moment is all you have...

Remember, it helps to have a pad and pencil in your pocket so that if you wish to remember any thoughts that arise you can jot them down to free your mind.

EXERCISE 18 – Sitting with water

Find yourself a pond, lake, stream, river, waterfall, sea, any water source.

Sit comfortably and begin to breathe slowly and deeply in and out to your stomach area.

Watch the water. See what is happening: reflections, movements, sounds etc.

Allow yourself to BE.

When your mind drifts, come back to breathing in and out, and your observation of the water.

Sit for at least 5 minutes and longer if you can.

EXERCISE 19 – Being with a tree/contemplating nature or a garden

Nature affords us wonderful opportunities to be Mindful.

Many people like to sit with their back to a tree or simply sit and look at the beauty of nature or a garden.

Be out in nature. Find yourself sitting comfortably and start to breathe deeply into your stomach area. Then ask yourself:

What can I see?

What can I hear?

What can I smell?

Is there a taste in my mouth?

What can I touch?

How do I feel?

Come back again and again to the present moment and if your mind starts to drift, place your attention on the area between your neck and your groin and breathe slowly and deeply in and out to your stomach area. Use your breath to stay present.

EXERCISE 20 – What do I want?

At the end of a relationship we can be left empty, bereft and confused. We can be so empty we no longer know who were are or what we want. This exercise helps you to focus so that you can come back to yourself.

Ensure that you have a notepad and a pen next to you.

Sit in a comfortable position and go through the steps in **Exercise 2.**

Then, imagining that there is a slit on the top of your head, post the question: "What do I want?" Write down whatever arises. If nothing arises, then write 'nothing'.

Then stand up and shake yourself off, sit down and compose yourself again, breathing deeply in and out and when you are ready, pose the question for a second time.

Repeat this exercise for a third time. Be kind to yourself.

EXERCISE 21 – Visualising a place of wellness

This exercise is one where we take ourselves elsewhere than where we are – which is not the usual 'paying attention to where we are'. However, being able to visualise a place where we feel well is a useful tool to have when we feel stressed or low.

Sit or lie in a comfortable place. Check your body and how it feels. Adjust your position if you have any discomfort. Now think of a place in which you feel really well: a place which is special to you. If you do not have such a place in your present or past, then imagine one by inventing it or thinking of a place you would like to visit.

Close your eyes. Breathe deeply into your stomach area. Relax. Allow thoughts to arise, display and dissolve without engaging with them. Come back to your breath every time you find you are drifting away with a thought. Then ask yourself, slowly and deliberately, taking your time:

What can I see?....................

What can I hear? ....

What can I smell? ....

Is there a taste in my mouth? ....

What can I touch? ....

How do I feel? ....

This is your special place, your place of wellness. Relax as you imagine yourself there, for as long as you wish, breathing into your stomach area. Then gently imagine the place shrinking into a very small jewel, and take it into your heart. This is a place to which you can return any time you wish. It is especially good if you awake in the middle of the night and need some comfort.

EXERCISE 22 – Mindfully listening to music

We all have music we like. Rarely do we Mindfully listen to it in our homes – it is often used as a background to whatever else we are doing.

Choose a piece of your favourite music. Go to a place in your home where you can relax, either sitting or lying down. Put on the music. Breathe deeply in and out to your stomach area. Now really HEAR the music. Allow your thoughts to arise, as they inevitably do and if you find yourself engaging with them, remind yourself that the music is your anchor.

Come back again and again to the sound, the tones, the way the music changes and the effect that it is having on your body, on your heart. Really FEEL it in you and allow yourself to enjoy it. Be fully present, fully alive, enjoying the music.

Do this for as long as you wish.

Use this technique whenever you go to a concert. Really BE with the music rather than allowing your mind to drift off with your thoughts.

EXERCISE 23 – Actively dealing with self-criticism

Having adequate resilience implies having the ability to withstand or recover from difficult situations. This in turn increases your resistance to depression. This exercise is inspired by the theory of Cognitive Behavioural Therapy. When an incident happens we give it a meaning: the meaning causes thoughts; the thoughts create feelings and emotions; the feelings and emotions dictate how we handle whatever arises. We can improve our self-compassion and self-esteem by weighing up our sweeping statements and allowing ourselves to have a more balanced view.

Sit calmly and comfortably with a pen and paper. Commence by breathing slowly and deliberately into your stomach area and be aware of the solidity of your body. Allow yourself time to arrive 'on the spot'.

Write down a sweeping statement that you have recently made about yourself, as a result of an incident: 'I am ....'.

Consider the negative emotion or emotions that you are holding in your mind and body as a result of this statement, write it/them down and give a score out of 10 for the intensity.

Then write down a list of reasons why the statement is true. Follow this with a list of reasons why the statement is NOT true. Make this list longer than the previous one!

Then create what, as a Buddhist, I call 'The Middle Way': Write a statement along the lines of "Sometimes I say that I am .... but this is because I am (sad, broken-hearted, feeling raw, lacking in self esteem.... etc) and when I look at the evidence for and against I realise when I talk to myself in this way it is because I am human and that nothing is black and white and therefore

....(write something here that shows how the sweeping statement is not 100% true and that it is mitigated by the list of why the statement is not true).

Score again the emotions that you scored in the beginning. Usually, the score will be lower, because you have reasoned with yourself and you realise that as a human being life involves suffering. It is unavoidable. What is important is that we allow our thoughts to come and go and *breathe* when we are feeling vulnerable or sad.

EXERCISE 24 – Use of triggers

The biggest obstacle to Mindfulness, by far, is the fact that we forget to remember to be Mindful! Anything that we can use to remind us is a good thing.

Decide what triggers you will be using to remind you to be Mindful. Is it having pet pebbles or crystals? Can you use an App on your phone so that it goes off on the hour? Could it be a decision that every time you see a certain colour you will remember to be Mindful? Or might it be a certain time of day – such as waking up or just before you go to sleep?

Whenever you are aware of your trigger, practice Mindfulness by using 3 Mindful breaths, breathing in a healing colour or any other short exercise that appeals to you.

EXERCISE 25 – Knowing yourself

Learning to love yourself involves checking in with yourself during the day to see how you are feeling. Negative self-talk will show up until you learn to be in a loving relationship with yourself.

At times during the day, ask yourself 'How am I feeling, right now?' You could be feeling stressed, relaxed or neutral. What thoughts, emotions, and feelings are present? Where in your body might you be holding these? You might want to ask yourself how these arose.

Remember that the stream flowing through our brain-mind is always present and that we, as the watcher of that stream, occasionally become aware of what the stream contains.

It could be that you have been talking harshly to yourself because of something that happened. Whatever is there, remember that thoughts are just thinking and that nothing stays the same. Thoughts lead to feelings which then show up in your body. Reminding yourself that this happens enables you to monitor yourself and know how your mind is working.

However you are, just remember to breathe deeply into your stomach area and allow yourself to come back to centre with an attitude of kindness and openness.

Do this several times a day, when you think about it.

EXERCISE 26 – Sitting with your morning coffee

People often say they do not have time to meditate. This short exercise will help you to get into a routine.

Make your morning drink and take it to your cushion/seat sitting somewhere pleasant (in front of your altar, some flowers, trees, water, whatever is suitable for you). Gently sip your drink as you breathe deeply into your stomach. Focus on enjoying the taste of your drink, the feeling of being in the moment, the way it feels to breathe deeply. Allow yourself to really relax. When you have finished your drink you may wish to follow with a five minute meditation practice.

Getting into a routine of starting the day in this way will be very beneficial to you and help you to deal with stress.

SECTION SEVEN

MORE INFORMATION AT THE END

"Your happiness lies within you"

Tibetan proverb

Jackie Hawken

Mad Cow*

For Jackie

My friend called me yesterday,
Needed to talk some of her pain away.
The love of her life's walking out.
Seven years together, but he 'needs to be free',
So she's a tad upset, understandably.
Built a life around him, thought they'd be wed,
Now a future alone fills her with dread.
She's a Mad Cow.

She's a passionate woman, this friend of mine,
Been up and down in her life, many a time,
Raised two kids, all on her own,
Worked really hard to buy her own home.
Justifiably proud of where she's at now,
She's a mum, a teacher and a professional
Mad Cow.

Now her plans are laid waste, her heart is sore,
Because the man she loves just walked out her door,
Feeling scared, alone, angry and more
I'm right there with her as she spills out the story,
Her feelings so vivid, all guts and glory,
Intensity, immensity, you know how it is,
These feelings of hers, I don't know about his.
She's a Mad Cow.

Seems that he's fine – buying a new place,
Moving soon as he can, can't hide his distaste
Of her rantings and ravings, tears and despair,

176

Dislikes her weakness... and her facial hair.
When she ripped up his letters, threw them over their
bed,
He looked bemused – 'Get a lodger' he said,
'Don't waste your time going over what's done
Sorrow's for fools – you need to move on.'
And she hears those words and looked at herself,
A wild-eyed woman, left on the shelf,
And saw a Mad Cow.

I saw my friend J, just the other week,
Composed, as always, slim and sleek.
You'd never guess that her life's a mess,
But I know the truth, I know she's been blessed
By a certain disease – we all know the name,
Makes you lose your reason, you go insane.
When in its grip, you scream in the wind,
You die a death, you just cave in
To the wild tides of feeling that break open your
heart,
Shut down your mind – and mind, it is an art
To ride these white waters of anger and pain,
I say again, it will send you insane.
This is not an affliction, nor is it a curse,
For I can conceive of nothing worse
Than to live a life in calm oceans
Untouched by emotions

For the 'path' in pathology is the same as in
sympathy,
It's our birthright to feel, to grieve and to rage,
Especially now, in this day and age,
It may not be a relationship falling apart,

Jackie Hawken

But how do you feel, how goes your heart,
With oil spills and landfills and factory farms,
With torture, rape and the race to arms?
You can say it's all right, it's all in the hands
Of the god or gods of our world, of our lands.

And I know it's 'OK', all will be well
With my friend J but, truth to tell,
I caught a glimpse of her wild woman, the other day
And it was magnificent, I have to say.
Not lovely, not pretty, not sure or well-kempt.
It was too fierce for that, and her veil was rent
Asunder.

And I stood in wonder
At her,
At myself,
At all of us here.

How would it be if we all dropped the fear,
And wept and wailed and roared, and more?
Laid our hearts open, messy and raw
In the moment, the present, the here and the now?
Channelling through our own
Mad Cow.

Cathi Pawson, 2010

*Cathi affectionately wrote this poem after I told her that during
the 'devaluation' stage of being in the relationship with the ex, I
felt like a 'mad cow' as he was constantly criticising me.

Recommended reading

Tara Brach – Radical Acceptance. 2003

Coleman Barks – The Essential Rumi. 1998

Jelaluddin Rumi (Author), Coleman Barks (Ed.) & John Moyne (Ed.) – This Longing. 2006

M. Williams, J. Teasdale, Z. Segal & J. Kabat-Zinn – The Mindful Way Through Depression. 2007

Jon Kabat-Zinn – Full Catastrophe Living. 1991

Jon Kabat-Zinn – Wherever You Go, There You Are. 1994

Thich Naht Hanh – You Are Here. 2001

Akong Tulku Rinpoche – Taming the Tiger. 1995

Akong Tulku Rinpoche – Restoring the Balance. 2005

Akong Tulku Rinpoche – Limitless Compassion. 2010

Lama Yeshe Losal – Living Dharma. 2001

Pema Chödrön – Comfortable with Uncertainty. 2004

Pema Chödrön – Start Where You Are. 2005

Pema Chödrön – When Things Fall Apart. 2007

H H The Dalai Lama – any of his books

Jackie Hawken

JACKIE HAWKEN

Jackie is a Mindfulness teacher, writer and psychological coach trained in Psychology, Law, Coaching, NLP, CBT, Mindfulness, Education and other disciplines. She has a passion for cooking, having worked as a cook in Greece, France, Italy and the UK as well as working as a medical researcher and lawyer before devoting her energies to the teaching of Mindfulness, self-esteem and coaching and to her writing career. This is her first book.

As a Buddhist, Jackie has more than thirty years' personal practice of meditation and Mindfulness She is based in Bristol, UK where she was born in 1952 and loves to take long walks with her beloved border collie – Alfie the Wonderdog.

www.mindfulnessbristol.co.uk
jackie.hawken@btinternet.com

Book synopsis

With wisdom and compassion, Jackie Hawken steers us through the Mindful journey of suffering to healing that can occur when a relationship, whether ordinary or toxic, ends. Sometimes we are left in great psychological pain and we must learn to choose between bitterness and acceptance. Accepting the journey of the dark night of the soul to finally be in a loving relationship with ourselves can be both liberating and empowering.

In order to properly heal, it is important to fully feel and acknowledge the negative emotions that can surface on these occasions: the first part of the book concentrates on this negativity. In the second part, we learn how to practise self-help, particularly by making the 26 user-friendly Mindfulness exercises a regular part of our daily lives.

40192434R00103

Made in the USA
San Bernardino, CA
13 October 2016